Dear Sophie

Life Lessons in
Feminism & Medicine

Dear Sophie

Dr. Ruth Simkin

BInk

Bink Books

Bedazzled Ink Publishing Company • Fairfield, California

978-1-949290-18-9 paperback

Cover Design
by

Bink Books
a division of
Bedazzled Ink Publishing, LLC
Fairfield, California
http://www.bedazzledink.com

To all the women who got us this far

And

To all the women who will lead us to true equality.

Acknowledgements

Many people have assisted in creating this book. As always, my first reader, literary colleague and good friend Dvora Levin has been there for me with her wonderful comments and suggestions. Her encouragement has kept me writing since we first met many years ago.

Much thanks and appreciation to Susan Holtz, an editor par excellence, whose superb assistance has helped bring this book into being. She is a wonderfully talented editor and I have been blessed with her involvement.

My memory needs as much help as it can get these days, and for assistance with remembering, I thank Dr. Jann Rogers, Marlene Conrad and Rob Krogseth. They have all jogged my memory to help bring you these stories. Special thanks to Jann for her reading and comments as well. Her encouragement has been more helpful than she can imagine.

Thanks to my family, as always, for being supportive, particularly sister Judi Simkin and cousin Maddy Santner. My brothers, sister, nieces, nephews and cousins are always there for me.

To keep my home running smoothly, I thank Chris Wilson for all things electronic and also for being the very best of friends; thanks to Sheila Hatswell for running the household and Marvin Kurier for all he does for me and the house; thanks to Estelle Kurier and family for being such an important part of my life; and thanks to Kelly for driving me nuts but nevertheless, causing me to laugh daily.

Much thanks and gratitude go to Bedazzled Ink Publishing—C.A. Casey, Claudia Wilde, and Liz Gibson. As we work more together, things become easier and easier and they are great publishers with whom to work. And thanks to Sapling Studio, C.A. Casey and Claudia Wilde, for the wonderful cover and bringing the book alive. I thank them all for everything they have done.

Author's Note

We experience life in our own unique ways. This is how I remember my life. Others who shared a similar path as I may have had different experiences. That would be their book to write. This is mine.

A Note on Feminism

For those who turn up their noses at the words feminists and feminism or scoff that feminism is an utterly pointless word, it might be beneficial to read this. The following list consists of six things a woman could not do in 1971.

In 1971 a woman could not:

1. Get a Credit Card in her own name—it wasn't until 1974 that a law forced credit card companies to issue cards to women without their husband's signature.
2. Be guaranteed that they wouldn't be unceremoniously fired for the offense of getting pregnant—that changed with the Pregnancy Discrimination Act of 1978.
3. Fight on the front lines—admitted into military academies in 1976, it wasn't until 2013 that the military ban on women in combat was lifted. Prior to 1973 women were only allowed in the military as nurses or support staff.
4. Take legal action against workplace sexual harassment. Indeed, the first time a court recognized office sexual harassment as grounds for any legal action was in 1977.
5. Decide not to have sex if their husband wanted to—spousal rape wasn't criminalized in all fifty states until 1993.
6. Obtain health insurance at the same monetary rate as a man. Sex discrimination wasn't outlawed in health insurance until 2010 and today many, including sitting elected officials at the Federal level, feel women don't mind paying a little more.

One last thing: prior to 1880, the age of consent for sex was set at ten or twelve in most states, with the exception of Delaware—where it was SEVEN YEARS OLD!

Feminism is NOT just for other women.
KNOW your HERstory.

Dear Sophie,

BY THE TIME you are able to read and understand this, I will likely no longer be on this earth. That is one of the reasons I am writing this to you. My life has been full, a life very different than the one you are likely to live. As you know, I didn't have children of my own. Your mother and her sister, my nieces, were important people in my life and I had the opportunity to spend much time with them both as they grew up. You are my grand-niece— or great-niece. I am not sure which is the correct term, but both sobriquets should fit you well.

I don't want my life to have been lived for naught—perhaps if I tell you about my experiences, you will extract some wisdom enabling you to lead your own life with greater clarity and ease. I want to share with you, not only some things I've learned during the incredible life with which I've been blessed, but also what the times were like for women during the second half of the last century. Needless to say, things were very different. I don't want to die without leaving behind my history. There are some things women should never forget or take for granted. This story is my gift to you and to myself. I hope reading it will assist you in living an intelligent, respectful life, carrying the souls of the women who preceded you in your heart.

I wasn't always a doctor. I chose a different path from most of my peers. Most of the girls I had gone to school with in the 1950s were married and many were happy in their domesticity. There was absolutely nothing wrong with that; it just wasn't my path. I've always believed it was important to have choices which lead to more opportunities. My life would be different.

It was 1969 and I was living in Rockville, Maryland. One particular day, I had just received my twenty-fifth rejection letter to attend medical school. I was sad and depressed, lying in the already-turned-cold bathwater, reviewing the letters in my head:

- You are too old (I was 25);
- You live in the United States (from the Canadian schools);
- You are a Canadian (from the U.S. schools);
- You were once in a mental hospital.

The mental hospital, mental hospital, mental hospital . . . That place was never going to leave my life. All I wanted was to become a physician, a good physician like my Dr. B., Dr. Frances Brennecke, the psychiatrist who had helped me leave that cursed mental hospital. I wanted to help people just as she had helped me. I didn't care where I went to school, as long as I could study medicine. After twenty-five rejections, I was despondent, not knowing what to do next.

In the next room, the radio was playing. This was long before the days of iPods and other electronics that played music. In fact, cassettes or CDs weren't even around yet. My home had a radio, a record player, and LPs. I started singing along with Donovan: "Jennifer, Juniper . . . la la la la la."

Suddenly, a thought popped into my head: "Wouldn't it be great to get a St. Bernard named Jennifer!" Where this idea came from is forever a mystery to me. I already lived with my toy poodle, Peppy, who came to college with me every day, where we usually attended classes together. She was smart and loving; I hadn't felt the need for another animal companion until Jennifer the St. Bernard popped into my head. If I have a St. Bernard, I reasoned, my life would change; if my life changed, perhaps I would then get into medical school.

Now, Sophie, I know that this makes no logical sense but sometimes we just have to go with what we've got. So, herein lies a lesson for you: trust your instincts. If it feels right, it probably is right, even if it seems illogical.

I felt so strongly that I should get a St. Bernard and name her Jennifer that I hopped out of the bathtub, quickly dressed, and pulled out the Yellow Pages, my best friends in those days. I was able to locate a St. Bernard breeder in Virginia and, within two weeks, Jennifer the St. Bernard pup came to live with me and Peppy. And my life changed forever.

Getting Jennifer was the very beginning of a brand new adventure in life for me. I had just needed to make that move, to kick-start myself into a new way of doing things. By this small act, I enabled myself to do things that might not follow logically, that were perhaps not expected, that might seem just a little crazy. In the long run, it all worked out perfectly. More or less.

FOUR WEEKS LATER, while Peppy and I were teaching Jennifer how to sit on command, my father telephoned me.

"I may have some good news for you, Ruthie."

"Oh?" I was cautious. My dad's idea and my idea of good news did not necessarily concur.

"You remember my friend Chick Thorseen? We were in construction together a few years back. Well, he's now Chancellor at that new University of Calgary. I was talking to him the other day, and he told me that the University was planning a new medical school."

"So? That's just one more place for me to get rejected from. Why is that good news?"

"He told me that this school was going to be different, not just how they teach, but in the students they accept. They are looking for a different kind of student. He thinks you should try talking to the new Dean of Medicine who has just moved to Calgary. You can call and make an appointment."

"Gee, I don't know, Dad. Why would he even wanna talk with me? When does this school start?"

"It starts next fall. You can apply. You have lots of time—over a year. Maybe you can even come back to Canada in the meantime."

"Gee, I don't know—I guess one more rejection won't make that much difference . . ."

"Think positive. Maybe this is the school for you. I think you should make an appointment to talk to that dean. And after you see him in Calgary you can come to Winnipeg for a visit. We miss you a lot, you know."

"I guess it wouldn't hurt to talk to the guy. I'm not sure what good it will do, but . . ."

"Atta girl. Give it a try. You never know."

"'kay, Dad, I'll see if I can get an appointment with him. Thanks for the tip. And thank Mr. Thorseen too. Love ya' all. Bye."

I made an appointment to meet with Dr. Bill Cochrane, the founding Dean of Medicine at the University of Calgary. I decided to drive to Calgary with Peppy and Jennifer, have the interview, and then stop in Winnipeg to introduce Jennifer to my family. She was a good puppy: smart, loveable, beautiful, and very amusing. She was only three months old but she was huge. Peppy was about the size of Jennifer's head.

The two dogs got along splendidly and we were a happy family unit.

I ARRIVED IN Calgary and checked into a motel near the university. I didn't know one single soul in the city. The following day, I stood in front of a mirror before heading off to meet the dean.

"Is this what a doctor-to-be should look like?" I asked my reflection. The plaid-skirted figure with beige blouse looked back at me and shrugged.

Here I was, trying yet again. But this year was different. I was only applying to one school, after more than two dozen rejections. There was nothing wrong with my marks—I had graduated from college *cum laude* with an A average—but still I received twenty-five identical responses to my applications: "Nope, no medical school for you." One has to have a lot of ego strength to withstand twenty-five rejections all within a period of a few months. Nevertheless, I guess my ego was strong enough because I decided to try one last time. I wanted to be a doctor—every cell in my entire body ached with that desire, and I was now hoping that Calgary would be the place.

When I looked into the mirror, a young woman looked back at me. She had short brown silky hair, very fine, like baby's hair, which, now that it was freshly washed, blew up in filmy strands around her head. Not a bad look, I thought with a smile. I turned to the side to make sure my blouse was tucked neatly into my plaid skirt. I felt that, for my first meeting with the dean, I should dress like someone serious about becoming a doctor. It would have been easy to know what to wear if I were a man but being a woman was more difficult. I didn't know very many women doctors. In fact, at that time, I didn't know any except for Dr. Brennecke, in Maryland, and Dr. Nona Doupe, my doctor from Winnipeg.

I had polished my brown loafers the evening before and now I hooked up my nylons. Ugh, it was hot, and I hated wearing pantyhose, but I thought wearing socks with loafers would be too juvenile. I had carefully planned my wardrobe, something I was not used to doing. I wanted to make a good impression, to appear relaxed yet serious, someone the Dean would trust, someone on whom he might take a chance.

"Okay, Ruth, off you go." I waved at my reflection. "You are not going to look any better or become any smarter by just standing here." I reckoned I felt as good as I possibly could, considering how incredibly nervous I was. I liked the woman I saw. I liked what she wore. I thought she looked like someone who could be a medical student, a good medical student who would turn into an excellent doctor. I petted the dogs goodbye and went off to meet the dean.

Sitting on a chair in a long hallway, the clamour of the hospital going on around me, I eagerly took everything in. This was a working hospital and I wanted to work in a place just like this.

I heard my name called and was shown into Dean Cochrane's office. Over the past year, I had gone to dozens of interviews with deans of medical schools and expected a pudgy, supercilious, aloof old coot. Instead, I was greeted by a grinning, handsome, fit young man with tousled sandy hair who rose to his height of six feet to offer his hand. He was casually yet elegantly dressed in blue slacks, sleeves rolled up on his light blue shirt. I liked him immediately.

"Good morning, Ruth. I am Dean Cochrane. As you see, everything is so brand new, we don't even have a building yet. That's why we're meeting here, in temporary offices. Sit down, sit down. Let's get to know one another. Tell me about yourself."

I told him why I wanted to go to medical school. He told me, very proudly, about the new school-to-be. Not only were they going to revolutionize how medicine was taught, they were going to accept a different breed of student. They were looking for "whole people who could bring a lot more to medicine than just good marks". As he spoke, I got more and more excited. It sounded exactly as though it was made for me: my ideal medical school.

I was very honest with the Dean. I liked him and felt safe with him. I told him about the mental hospital, how I had been admitted because of epilepsy, how I had been assigned a psychiatrist who was himself very mentally ill, and how it had taken more than a year and a half before that psychiatrist was relieved of his job and sent to his own mental hospital as a patient. I explained that my epilepsy was well controlled by medication and that, as soon as I had a proper psychiatrist, she and I started working on getting me released. The Dean understood that even ten years earlier, it was standard practice to admit patients with epilepsy into mental hospitals. These days, it was now considered a treatable neurological disease, not a psychiatric illness.

I described all the trouble I had had getting back into university because of my medical history but that, eventually, I had gone to Trinity College, graduated *cum laude*, and won an award from the Washington Chemical Society for discovering a physical constant. I told him I had then been rejected by two dozen medical schools in three countries.

"Well, Ruth, you understand, of course, that I cannot commit to anything. You will have to apply to medical school with everyone else and the selection committee will make its choice. But I can tell you that you are the kind of student we are looking for and I do encourage you to apply here."

I grinned so widely, I thought my lips would meet behind my head.

It was the summer of 1969 and Dean Cochrane suggested that, since the medical school wouldn't be starting for another year, I move to Calgary and take some courses at the University of Calgary during the 1969-70 school year.

"Take courses that appeal to you and apply to the medical school," he said. "We are only taking thirty-two students and we've already had hundreds of applications. The competition will be tough, you understand. I can't guarantee anything but I would encourage you to apply." He smiled kindly at me. I liked Dean Cochrane a lot and he seemed to like me too.

I left the office floating on air. I don't believe I had felt that good ever. Back at the motel, I changed my clothes, walked Peppy and Jennifer, and then we all hopped in the car and sang all the way to Winnipeg.

Two months later, I drove again to Calgary, this time to look for a place to live. And that is how I came to spend the next twenty-two years in Calgary, Alberta.

Well, Sophie, before I tell you about the mental hospital, let me back up even more. I had been a fairly wild teenager. I always fought with my dad and didn't fit in with the Jewish kids with whom my parents wanted me to hang out. I preferred the kids who played sports. In those days, the 1950s, "nice Jewish girls" didn't play sports. You know, Sophie, I played basketball all through junior high and high school and was Captain of the team for several years. I played basketball four years for the University of Manitoba.

My parents never, not once, ever saw me play or attended a game. It just was not what nice Jewish girls did. I did not want to be a nice Jewish girl, giggling whenever the boys looked her way. My relationship with my father was rather tumultuous those days.

When I was sixteen, I went to Los Angeles to visit some relatives over Christmas holidays. My aunt set me up on a blind date, a nice Jewish boy named Ricky. His sister, Annette, and her boyfriend, George, came out with us and we had a lot of fun. We saw each other every night of my visit and wrote to each other after I left. Ricky came to visit me in Winnipeg and for the next two years we spent as much time together as we could. I liked him well enough but I was still having fun being a teenager. So, I was very surprised when he asked me to marry him. When he said he wanted to talk with me, I actually thought he was going to break up with me.

"Marry me? Why would you want to marry me?" I asked. "I'm only seventeen."

"I love you, Ruthie. I'll wait until you feel you are old enough. But I want to marry you."

I remember sitting there thinking to myself, "Hmm, I've never been married before. Maybe I should give it a try."

"Sure, Ricky, I'll marry you." I smiled, thinking how happy it would make my parents to know that I was going to marry a nice Jewish boy. And it did make them happy. Everyone was just thrilled. Finally, I would be a nice Jewish girl after all and marry a nice Jewish boy like I was supposed to. When I finally came to my senses and realized that I didn't really love Ricky—he was nice enough, but I certainly didn't love him—I told him, my parents, his parents, everyone I could that I did not want to get married.

"Nonsense, dear, it's just nerves," I was told.

"Of course you want to get married. Don't be silly."

"You'll see how happy you will be. Don't worry."

Well, we got married. Maybe I was a bit blind, but I sure couldn't see happiness anywhere in the imminent future. Ricky wanted to marry a nice Jewish girl alright: one who cooked his dinner, did his laundry, and cleaned his house. I was also in third year at University of Manitoba with a double major and I resented ironing his underwear when I wanted to be studying. But, I continued trying to be a nice Jewish girl until I found out that he wasn't even going to school at all. He was playing poker in his cousin's garage all day. And losing, too. I kicked him out of our apartment. He went back to California. My dad made me go back to get him and bring him home.

"You'll see, Ruthie," he reassured me, "once Ricky comes home everything will be just fine."

Well, it wasn't. I wanted to go to school and learn and he wanted to be rich without doing any work. I kicked him out again. This time, I would not listen to my father about bringing him back. In fact, it took five years to get a divorce. In those days, you had to prove grounds like adultery or desertion and Ricky did not want to give me a divorce easily.

In the meantime, I was twenty years old, in fourth year at university and getting into more and more trouble with my parents. I was also in trouble with the police. I was having blackouts and did not know why. I had a bad car accident where I had been acting crazy. While I did imbibe a sufficient amount in those days, that particular evening, I had not been drinking at all. The police arrested me for drunk driving because they found wine in my car and because I was acting like a drunk person. In short, I met with an officer of the court, told her what had happened, she told the judge, and he gave me a suspended sentence with the condition that I receive a medical investigation. I was very happy to do that because I had been puzzled by my actions, not understanding them at all. I went to the Winnipeg General Hospital Psychiatric Ward for an assessment. There I met one of my true saviours: Dr. Nona Doupe. She discovered I had epilepsy and had been having temporal lobe seizures. I was delighted with this discovery because it now meant there was an explanation for my actions and, more importantly, treatment. My parents were not so delighted. In the 1960s, a diagnosis of epilepsy, considered a psychiatric disease in those days, was equivalent to the very worst psychiatric disorder a person could have. My parents were mortified. They immediately wanted a second opinion. I, on the other hand, just wanted to get treated and finish my fourth year at University.

Because my parents were so deeply upset with this diagnosis, I agreed to go away with them just for a week-end consultation at Menninger's Clinic in Kansas, then considered one of the finest psychiatric hospitals in the world. We were to leave on a Friday, see a doctor there on Saturday, and return home Sunday. I didn't come back home for over two years.

The doctor there told my parents I needed psychiatric care but they did not have a bed. She then sent us to Maryland to another hospital there where I was assigned a psychiatrist who was himself less than healthy, a fact subsequently confirmed by the other doctors there. It took over a year until the doctors in charge agreed to let me see another therapist. Finally, I met my other saviour, Dr. Frances Brennecke, who felt I did not belong there and worked hard to get me out as quickly as possible. I was a patient there just over two years when I was finally discharged and continued to see Dr. B., as I called her, privately.

Even though most people at the hospital thought I would be a "lifer," I never believed that, not even for a second, because I always saw myself back in school. Getting out of there was my temporary problem. Sophie, I think one's state of mind is critical to our outcomes, along with a lot of resilience in a tough world. I went into the hospital knowing that I would come out just fine and so everything that happened to me there, and a lot did, was just potholes and bumps on the road to leaving. My grandmother, my mother's mom, once told me we could always be free. When I questioned her, she pointed to her head. "Be free here," she told me, tapping her finger on her temple, "and no one can ever own you." That's a very good lesson to remember. In 2010, I wrote a book about my experiences in that mental hospital. I'm delighted to say that the book, *The Jagged Years of Ruthie J.* got excellent reviews and did quite well.

But back in the 1960s, all I wanted was to go back to school. However, no school would take me because I had been in a mental hospital. Finally, I talked my way into a junior college nearby, took three courses, got three A+'s and tried to get into university. Any university. And there were dozens in the area. No one would have me.

One day, feeling particularly depressed, I told Dr. B. that I was starting lab tech school. I really wanted to become a doctor, but no university would admit me. That was the only time she ever got involved in my personal life. She called a friend of hers who worked at Trinity College in Washington, D.C. who arranged for me to meet with the Mother Superior to see if she would let me attend their university. I guess the Mother Superior liked me because, the next thing I knew, I was the sole Jew at a Catholic university of over fifteen hundred women. I loved it there and got an undergraduate degree in science.

When I first got out of the hospital and moved into my own apartment, I took the bus to see Dr. Brennecke and really didn't go to many other places. But once I started back at school, I needed a car: I lived in Bethesda,

Maryland; Dr. B. was in Rockville, Maryland: my first school was in Chevy Chase, Maryland; Trinity College was in Washington, DC. Everything was not too far with a car, but would be many hours up and back on a bus.

I discussed this at length in detail with my dad. I definitely wanted a convertible. In fact, I am now in my seventies and until this very year have always had a convertible. Sometimes I have had two cars, like a sports car convertible and a bigger car for large dogs and other large things. But always a convertible. I loved driving with the top down, even in winter. If it wasn't snowing or raining, the top was down. I probably would have preferred a foreign car, but my father persuaded me to go with General Motors. That made him happy and just having a convertible, any convertible really, would make me happy too.

I walked into the Buick salesroom. I knew exactly which model I wanted and how much it should cost. A salesman looked at me.

"What do you want?" he asked, none too nicely.

"I would like to buy this model of Buick convertible." I smiled, pointing to my car of choice sitting in the showroom.

He laughed. "Come back with your father, girlie." He snorted, and walked away.

I stood there for a moment, realized he was not coming back, so I left and went to the next Buick dealer on the Rockville Pike. The salesman there was as nice as could be and, in no time flat, I had my new car. The very first place I drove, top down of course, was back to the first car dealership. I stopped outside the door, beeped the horn several times, and, when the first salesman looked out, I shouted, "This could have been your sale!" Then I honked again and drove off, leaving him standing there with his mouth open so wide that a large bird could have nested in it.

Now, Sophie, there will be times in your life when people, mostly men, will not take you seriously. Don't let them get away with it. Do what you came to do, with or without their help. Don't ever let anyone tell you that you can't do something or have something because you are a woman.

I had my car, I graduated *cum laud* from Trinity College, now all I had to do was get into a medical school, which, so far, was not proving easy. Medical schools typically chose students who look as though they will succeed. On paper, I appeared a huge risk, even though my grades were stellar.

1969-70
The Year Before Medical School

WHEN I FIRST moved to Calgary, I was thrilled to be back in Canada. I had lived in the United States through five difficult years: John F. Kennedy's assassination had occurred just months prior to my arrival and, during my time in the US, both Bobby Kennedy and Martin Luther King had been assassinated and pervading everything was the Vietnam War. Everyone I knew was personally and deeply affected by that war.

There was violence in my daily life, too. When I volunteered in the emergency room at Howard University, in the black area of Washington, D.C., I had to be escorted to my car in the parking lot by security—they would not let me go outside alone. One night, someone came into the emergency room, gun spewing bullets all around. I crouched on the floor under the desk until the shooter was subdued. I ached for calm, gun-less, war-less Canada. I was ready to come home.

In Calgary, I found a realtor who helped me find the perfect home. It was a little log cabin sitting on three acres atop a hill, not too far from the hospital and actually within the city limits. There were only four other houses on the hill and lots of open space. I adored it. It was funky, had character, and was very beautiful to my eye.

My father, your great-grandfather, was appalled by my preference. He had been in construction, building nice housing developments with nice yards for nice people on nice streets—exactly the kind of place that was anathema to me. He could not understand how I could possibly give up a nice house with all the nice amenities for a little log cabin.

"At least look at Lake Bonavista," he urged. "We could get you a good deal there and the houses are brand new."

He insisted on driving me out to the housing development. Inside each house, I would run up to the window that faced west and look out wistfully toward my little log cabin sitting atop its hill overlooking the city. I did not want to live in a sterile house in a housing development with an avocado coloured oven.

I took my dad back to the little log cabin. He was very angry.

"This house will fall down—look at it!" He kicked at the wooden siding. "It's poorly made, it's all alone out here with no neighbours. What will a single girl like you do out here? This is silly, Ruthie, you are doing something very silly."

"Look, Dad, it's perfect for me. It's quiet, I can study. It's great for the dogs. The only two things I want to do is be a doctor or be a farmer. If I don't get into medical school, I can just buy some land up on this hill and learn how to farm. Across the street from here is a seventeen acre lot for sale. I don't know anything about medicine or farming and I'll have to learn something new anyway. This is where I want to live."

I secretly hoped I would not have to buy that acreage.

"I think you are making a big mistake. A big mistake. But it's your life and your money. If you want to live here, that's your choice, but I'm telling you it's the wrong choice." We argued and argued but, in the end, it was my money and my decision and the little log cabin won over. It wasn't so little anyway. This was the first time I defied my dad in anything related to business or money. I knew in my guts that this log cabin was to be my home.

Many years later, I was offered two and a half million dollars for my property, more than fifty times what I had originally paid; I refused the offer because I loved living there too much to move. My father would brag about what a brilliant businesswoman his daughter was, having found this priceless piece of property. I guess he forgot all the fights we had about it. I didn't care about the fights. I just wanted to live there. And live there I did—for twenty-two eventful and interesting years.

When I finally did get into medical school, and didn't have to consider buying land and learning how to become a farmer, I had been living in my log cabin for a year and was loving it more every day. I was very happy about the way things turned out because I think I made a much better doctor than I would have been a farmer. Decades later, I did try farming for several years. Although I was reasonably successful, I missed medicine terribly and went back to it. But that's another story.

One of the first things I did once I moved in was to plant a vegetable garden. I had rows of carrots and lettuce and all sorts of wonderful veggies. But the potatoes—ah, the potatoes were my special project. I planted them very carefully, so that when they came out of the ground, they spelled, in letters four feet high and three feet wide: FUCK. Why? I did that so when they were ready to eat and we were sitting at the table, I could say, "Pass the fuckin' potatoes please." I thought that was very funny. Obviously, my sense of humour was still fairly underdeveloped. But the potatoes became famous. People in small planes and hot air balloons would swoop down to read the potatoes, which I kept very neatly weeded so the letters were clear as could be. They brought me a lot of pleasure, both in looking and later on, in eating.

After spending years locked up in the mental hospital and four more years studying in a Catholic university surrounded by nuns in full drag, the sense of freedom I experienced on my three acres in my log cabin was intoxicating. I loved my home. I would sit outside with Peppy and Jennifer and just grin. Just outside the cabin on the other side from the garden was a poplar grove and I would often sit among the trees, elated with the good fortune in my life. I was back in university, which I loved, and I had a chance to get into a medical school. I was living free, in exactly the kind of place that suited me. The house was a real log cabin. There was a large fireplace in the living room, one large bedroom and another smaller one, a fine kitchen with bar stools beside a counter, and a dining room. It couldn't have been more ideal. The living room was the largest room in the house, with one whole wall of windows that overlooked the city from high up on the hill. I felt like the luckiest person in the world.

I SIGNED UP to take courses at the University of Calgary, as the dean had suggested, and I was enjoying them a lot. I had gone to the University of Manitoba almost four full years studying English, Philosophy, and Psychology, and then subsequently completed an undergraduate degree in sciences at Trinity College in Washington, D.C. In Calgary, I was heavy into the biochemistry courses. I had to show how well I could do when compared to all the others applying to medical school. The competition was fierce.

One day, due to an unexpected traffic jam, I was unavoidably twenty minutes late for a class. When it was over, I turned to Marla, the woman seated next to me, and asked if I could see her notes from the part I had missed.

Marla pulled her dark hair away from her face and looked up at me with a puzzled expression on her face.

"No, I can't give you my notes. Everyone in this class is applying for medical school. What if I help you and then you beat me out and I don't get in? Sorry." She picked up her notebook and walked out.

"Wow." I was really stunned by Marla's reaction. That attitude was distasteful to me and, as it turned out, also to some others.

"That was something else," Mickey said. He had been sitting on my other side and heard the discussion. "You can see my notes if you like."

"And mine, too, but they're not so great," Ron added, who was sitting behind us.

"Look, let's make a deal, right now," Mickey said. "The three of us will always share our notes and any other information with each other. Like the three musketeers. Okay?"

"Absolutely okay." I smiled.

"I'm in." Ron grinned.

Mickey put out his hand, I put mine on top, then Ron.

"One for all and all for one," the three of us said in unison, and then burst out laughing.

Mickey, Ron, and I very quickly became good friends. It seemed the imminent opening of the medical school-to-be was all anyone ever talked about. The competition for the school was insanely challenging. Imagine, over twelve hundred people were competing for thirty-two spaces.

Ron was a nursing supervisor at Foothills Hospital; he was married with six children and a decade older than I. He was lankily slender with a curl of brown hair hanging over his forehead, and spoke with a mellifluous British accent. A year younger than I, Mickey was single, funny, bright, and gentle. The three of us bonded very quickly. We became lab and study partners, agreeing to help and support each other. We all fiercely wanted to become doctors and, as it turned out, we all succeeded without ever being nasty or competitive with the other students. Our friendship continued well beyond school, although, unfortunately, Ron is no longer with us.

I don't know what happened to Marla but she certainly never showed up at my medical school. I've thought about that incident with Marla often and it taught me something, Sophie. I believe if the situation would have been reversed, and Marla would have asked for my notes, I would have given them to her without a second thought. I actually felt sorry for her because she was in a position where she felt she couldn't do that. I believe she thought that this "killer competitiveness" was expected of her. I would hope she was kinder inside herself. Maybe she felt she couldn't be kind. So Sophie—always be true to yourself. I hope you never find yourself in the position of acting in a way that you feel is expected by others but that makes you uncomfortable. Inside you is a beautiful person and you owe it to yourself and to all those who love you to be as true to your essence as possible.

I WAS LONELY. With his wife and kids and work, Ron did not have an excess of free time. Mickey also worked a lot. I was also realizing that I was a lesbian, or at least bisexual, and I wanted to meet people who were more like me.

One day, I found a telephone number on a bulletin board at the university. I can't remember exactly what it said, but I knew it was a contact number for gays and lesbians. In those days, we didn't mention or write those words: "gays" or "lesbians." We had code words and expressions, like, "friend of Dorothy," or "member of the family" or "did you read *The Well of Loneliness?*" There were ways to find each other, but they were often convoluted ways.

I nervously dialed the telephone number.

"Hello," a cheerful voice answered. "Laurie here."

"Uh, hi. Er, I'm kinda new in town, um, I don't really know . . ."

"Oh, would you like to meet some lesbians and gay men?" she quickly asked.

I exhaled with relief. "Yes, yes, I would, but I don't know where to go."

"No problem." I could feel her smile over the telephone. "Just meet me on Friday night at the corner of 12th Avenue and 1st Street SW at nine o'clock. Okay?"

"12th and 1st. Friday night. Nine pm. Okay. Uh, what do you look like?"
She laughed. "You'll know. I'll find you."

Friday night came. Years later, I came to appreciate how Calgary was designed into quadrants and how the streets were numbered but that night, still new to the city, I was very late because somehow I ended up on a NE street instead of a SW avenue. I was upset and frustrated when I finally pulled up to the right corner. I saw a woman pacing.

"Hi! I thought you weren't coming." She smiled at me.

"Oh, I got so lost—first I went to the wrong streets, and then the wrong direction and I couldn't find the right place . . ."

"Never mind, you're here now. I'm Laurie. Come with me." She slipped her arm through mine. I looked over at this wonderful woman. She was beautiful: short blonde hair, a few inches taller than me, slim, strong, and with a perpetual smile on her face. She reminded me of a happy mischievous pixie and I felt good in her company.

Together we walked down a dark flight of stairs, pushed open a heavy door, and entered Club Carousel, the place that was to be my second home for many years.

Laurie walked me around, introducing me to pretty much everyone in the place. Men and women were sitting around talking, some were dancing, and almost everyone seemed happy. We settled at a table where two men and two women sat.

"Joanne, Cory, this is Ruth. Ruth, Joanne and Cory. And this is Rob and Ian. Ruth."

Everyone waved and smiled. I immediately felt welcome.

"Ruth is trying to get into medical school next year," Laurie offered.

"Oh really?" Joanne asked. "I am going to apply the year after that."

"No kidding? What are you doing now?"

"I work as a respiratory technologist. Cory and I live together."

Cory smiled, her red hair framing her huge green eyes. "Yes," she piped up, "and we are having a party next Saturday at our house and would love you to come. Would you?"

"I would love to. If I don't get lost." I smiled at Laurie.

"Well, it looks as though you are set," Laurie stood up. "I see someone over there I should go talk to. I'll see you next week at the party, okay?"

"Okay, thanks, Laurie, for everything. Really. I truly appreciate your help."

"No prob. Be cool." And off she went to initiate future conquests, leaving me with the four people who would become my best friends for the next six years.

RON WORKED AS a Nursing Supervisor and Mickey and I would often meet him at the hospital just to soak up the ambience.

"Ruthie, Mickey, guess what?" Ron was clearly excited.

"What? You found out something about medical school?" Mickey asked.

Ron smiled. "No. This hot shot plastic surgeon is coming to give a lecture to the doctors tomorrow night. I'm working that night so I can get you both into the lecture. C'mon. It'll be like we're real doctors. I'll get white coats for all of us."

The next night we were in the audience, attired in white coats, playing doctor. The guest speaker was indeed a plastic surgeon who was talking about the latest techniques in face lifts and other facial surgery. I didn't understand a lot of what he said but he had slides. A lot of slides. A lot of slides that were very close-up surgical photographs. I had no idea what I was seeing except it was a bunch of skin pulled back and muscles and blood and . . . I watched the first few and grabbed Ron's arm.

"Ron, I don't feel so good."

The next thing I knew, I was lying on the floor in the lobby, with Ron and Mickey hovering over me, wiping my face. I looked up at them.

"You fainted." Ron smiled. "You're okay. Just lie still for a while."

"Fainted? They'll never let me into medical school now." I felt the tears run down my face.

"Ruthie, listen, it's always a bit difficult the first time people see pictures like that. It's okay. Nobody even noticed," he lied. "Here, sit up, have some water."

I was so embarrassed, I couldn't even talk. How could I become a doctor if I couldn't even watch a lecture on facial reconstruction? Ron put his arm around me and gently gave my shoulders a squeeze. "You're fine, sweetie, you are. Don't worry about it."

I did though. I did worry about it. But that was the only time I ever fainted in all my years of training. You know, Sophie, life is often full of surprises and I think the best way to deal with them is to just let them happen. Like fainting. I was silly to worry about that. Worrying about insignificant things like that just takes our energy away from where we need it to be.

I WENT TO the party at Joanne and Cory's, and met a lot more people. On Friday nights we would gather at Club Carousel and, on Saturdays, someone had a house party, usually with lots of dancing. Because I had such a great place, with lots of space and privacy, my little log cabin was a frequent location for these parties. There were all kinds of events going on at Club Carousel, too. We put on plays and reviews and had costume parties. Unfortunately, we often met with hostility on the stairs leading down to the club. Young men would gather nearby and, when they saw us going down, they would throw stones at us, yelling, "Faggots, dykes, die!" We were young, and only a little scared, so we laughed at them, gave them the finger, and dodged the stones as best we could on our way down to our not-so-secret hangout.

By the end of that first year, I had amassed a large circle of friends. Both my social and academic lives were intense and joyous. My life was very full.

IT WAS NOW early spring and I was loving my life, although I was very nervous about getting accepted to medical school. The doorbell rang, followed by the sound of the door opening. I went into the hallway to see who had arrived. I always left my door unlocked, as people were constantly dropping in.

"I got in, look, luv, here it is, my acceptance." Ron grinned, waving a piece of paper.

"Oh, Ron, that's just great!" I gave him a big hug.

"I know your mail doesn't come until the afternoon, so I decided to keep you company while you wait for the post."

We knew the letters were coming out that day. Thirty-two people were going to be in the first year of Calgary's brand new medical school. Thirty-two people out of well over one thousand two hundred who had applied. And Ron was one of them. Would I be another?

We went into the kitchen where I put on a fresh pot of coffee. Ron sat on a stool and leaned on the counter, facing me.

"What about Mickey? When does his mail arrive?"

"Not until the afternoon," I answered. "Like me."

As I poured Ron's coffee, I reminded him of the first time the three of us did the three musketeers thing. He nodded and picked up a cribbage board from the counter.

"C'mon, let's go. We'll play cribbage while we wait for the mail."

"Oh, Ron, I don't know. I'm too nervous. I can't even think straight, much less count to twenty-one."

"Good. That means I'll finally beat you. C'mon, luv, let's get your mind off the mail."

He put his hand on my back and gently pushed me forward into the living room. He plunked down heavily on the orange shag carpet.

I liked my home. In fact, I loved my home. It never failed to please me, even at such a nerve-wracking time, as I sat down on the floor beside him.

"Fifteen two, fifteen four and a pair is six. What've ya' got, luv?"

"Huh? Sorry, my mind was elsewhere. Look, let's talk about you—aren't you excited?"

"We can talk about me later. I already had my excitement at home when I opened the mail. Then my wife went to work and the kids went off to school and, after I did my little jig, I came over here."

Ron put out his cigarette in the bean bag ashtray on the floor beside him. I had not smoked for two years. I didn't really want to smoke any more. But Ron smoked a lot and sometimes I was very tempted.

"What time is it now?"

"Asking that every five minutes is not going to make the time go any faster, luv. The mail will get here when it gets here." Ron reached for another cigarette, held out the pack to me, I took one, put it in my mouth, and he lit both our cigarettes. We sat there in silence, puffing for a few moments.

"Hey! Wait. What am I doing? I don't smoke. At least, not anymore."

"I guess you do now." He laughed.

And that is how I came to smoke for the next seven years.

"Did you hear something? Did you hear that?"

"Maybe," he said. "Perhaps the mail came."

I got up from the floor and ran to the front door. There indeed was the mail. I brought the stack of letters into the house and put them on the counter. Ron was right behind me.

And there it was. The distinctive logo from the University of Calgary Medical School. The letter. The letter that would define my life from then on. I held it in my trembling hands, afraid to open it. Yea or nay? I couldn't tell by holding the letter.

"C'mon, luv, open it up. Let's see what it says."

"I can't. I'm scared."

Ron laughed. "You've been waiting for this letter all day. Here it is. Wait's over. Open 'er up. C'mon, time to see, one way or the other."

My hands shook. I sat down. Very gingerly, I slid my finger under the flap and gently lifted it. I pulled out the one page letter and slowly unfolded it. Ron was looking over my shoulder. And there it was. ". . . pleased to inform you of your acceptance for the study of medicine . . ."

The tears surprised me. I laughed, wiping the wetness off my cheeks. I couldn't speak for a minute. I really did feel overwhelmed.

"Gotta call my parents," I said.

"I'll open a bottle of wine," Ron said.

"Great. And we should call Mickey too. I guess it's party time tonight."

Even though Mickey was not one of the thirty-two, he still came over to celebrate with us. Both Ron and I were deeply disappointed that he didn't get in—we had really wanted the three musketeers to go the distance together. As it turned out, he went to another medical school, became a doctor and, currently, is doing amazing humanitarian work in third world countries. I have always been incredibly proud of him and his work.

The little log cabin had filled up with people. I never understood how this happened and it never failed to amaze me; my house overflowed with people at the first sign of a celebration. And often at no sign at all. But that night was special. I was going to be a doctor.

Medical school at last. And I was here in my home, my wonderful log cabin, living with two amazing dogs, surrounded by friends celebrating with me. I was one incredibly lucky and joyous person.

1970-1971
First year of medical school

MEDICAL SCHOOL AND feminism entered my life at about the same time, which was somewhat ironic, since at that time they combined considerably less smoothly than oil and water. Almost from the beginning of my first year of medical school, I was involved in one embroilment or another with the staff and male students. It never occurred to me that being a woman in medical school would be a problem. In retrospect, that was very naïve of me.

I have always enjoyed being the first—the first of anything. This usually comes with a lot more responsibility, because one's actions help create a new reality. It is thrilling to help form a new entity. I was told that the University of Calgary wanted to build a new kind of medical school, one that cared about people and neither staff nor graduates were to be stereotypical doctors. This was exhilarating and I loved the idea that I could be a part of changing medicine for the better. I took my job as a first-year student in a brand-new medical school very seriously.

Here's something for you to consider, Sophie: If you ever have the chance to do something stimulating, exciting, and different, then go for it. Don't hold back because the way might be longer or more difficult. It will likely be worth it. Keep in mind the word "tenacity" and don't give up on getting what you want. Dare to become different.

I know that parts of this story will be pretty unbelievable, but trust me—it all happened. I know because I lived it.

That first day was one of the most exciting days of my life. I took the elevator up to the twelfth floor of Foothills Hospital, turned left, and immediately turned left again into an empty cavernous room. It wouldn't be empty for long; soon the cadavers and displays would be coming.

Along one wall were eight groupings, each with four desks in a U-shape. Beyond these quadratics was a door leading to offices and a lecture room, which had thirty-five chairs, each with a small desk/table attached. The chairs could be moved to form a circle for discussions or in lines facing the blackboard for a lecture. It was not fancy but it was soon home and we loved it.

Ron and I wandered toward the end of the long room and took the second-last quadratic before the back door. We were joined by Ron's friend, Paul. John took the fourth desk. We all knew each other, at least slightly, from the previous year's studies at the University. John was the good-looking jock, affable and easy going. This was to be our little family for the next few years.

I believed that we had all come to this first class of the University of Calgary Medical School to make a difference in society's perceptions of what defined a doctor. We were going to be different, to be better: respectful, honest, open— kind of a cross between Dr. Marcus Welby and Gandhi, holy, almost, in our belief that doctors could treat people differently, more respectfully than they had been. We were the beginning of the new breed of physicians. Or so I thought.

Our school was unique in other ways. Instead of having courses such as anatomy or physiology taught separately, we learned whole systems. For example, when we started the cardiovascular system, which includes the heart, all the blood vessels and everything else related to that system, we studied the anatomy and the physiology of that system, diseases, treatment, and everything that could possibly be related to the cardiovascular system. Then we moved on to the next system. I liked this way of learning because it put things in context immediately. We saw patients from the very first day of medical school. Some of these early patients had a very profound effect upon me and I still think about them.

I especially remember one patient who had ALS, amyotrophic lateral sclerosis. It's a terrible disease that affects nerve cells and leads to death often in less than two years. There is no cure yet. The patients' muscles weaken, ultimately ending in paralysis; they can't speak clearly, can't swallow, and ultimately, can't breathe. This woman was still able to sit upright on her own, but her speech was very difficult to understand. She was in her late fifties or early sixties. I think she had once been good looking, and was still elegant, even in her diseased state. She took hold of my arm and said urgently, "You find a cure for this. Don't let others die like this. You must help us." I nodded. What else could I do? I had only been in medical school a couple of weeks.

Of course, I wanted to make her better, somehow, but that was not possible. "Don't forget me," she rasped. I have not forgotten.

Our schedules were also different. Most medical schools were four years long with summers off, and then the graduates did their residencies. Our school was going to be three intense years of school, then straight into residencies. No summers off. I liked this idea a lot and looked forward to getting into it.

There were thirty-two of us, twenty-eight men and four women. The women—what a disparate group we were! Carol, married with a young child at home, lasted less than a year. Debbie was an eighteen-year-old music major who should have still been back in high school. She never seemed to know what was going on around her and I don't believe she ever did end up practicing medicine. She was definitely "on-paper intelligent" but as for "ways-of-the-world intelligent"—not so much. Thirdly, beautiful, blonde-haired Barb, who was a hard-working, conscientious, and obedient student who eventually became a very good pathologist. She immediately hooked up with John and stayed with him throughout our studies.

And who was I? I was definitely one of the older students—twenty-six years old when I started medical school. My past was colourful and complicated. My present was as well, I reckoned. I now lived with another woman, Joanne, who had left Cory and moved into my place, although Cory often lived with us as well. My home became party central for the school in the early days. I did not have close neighbours and the log cabin was less than fifteen minutes away from the hospital and medical school. We would gather in the log cabin, talk, eat, sometimes study, and generally bond through our shared experiences of becoming doctors. There was one group who smoked dope and there were the drinkers, who also came by several times a week. Also, of course, there were the frightened and confused—they showed up often. I struggled to save at least one night just for studying. However, it soon became necessary to study most evenings and party a lot less.

I NOTICED IT right from the beginning. I couldn't believe I was the only one who was bothered by it, but it seemed as though that was so. All the guys put pin-ups above their desks. In the 1960s and 1970s, Playboy pin-ups were de rigueur; they were a reasonably tame form of soft porn, but I found them offensive. The women in the photographs were almost nude and were suggestively posed. I had the periodic table over my desk. The guys often started the day by talking to or about these photos, mostly torn from Playboy Magazine. They debated the qualities of these women who were blatantly sharing their bodies with the rest of the world, belying the fact that our group was to become a different type of doctor.

"Oh, I would love to get between those legs," Howard said with a sneer one morning. His shifty eyes were his most distinctive feature and his pinched mouth did not soften the callous look on his face.

"Oh, I know just what you mean," Brian added with a grin, coming over with him from the next quadratic. "I had something like those two big bazookas last night myself."

I found Howard and Brian to be particularly repulsive. Often after making remarks like that, they would sneak a look at me to see if they had sufficiently raised my hackles. They had of course, but I would never let them see that. I ignored them and pretended not to care.

But I did care. I truly felt that this was to be a new-world medical school, one that showed respect for patients, doctors, and even medical students, not to mention the almost naked women. One morning, I joined the conversation.

"Hey, c'mon, you guys, that's disgusting. It's not at all respectful to those women."

I nodded toward all the pin-ups over the guys' desks. I felt as though my fellow students had defiled our study space. They all laughed at me.

It was only the first month of medical school and we were still getting settled in our new home away from home. And it wasn't just the male students.

The next week, one of the professors started his lecture on calcium metabolism by showing slides of naked, sexualized women.

"Now that I have your attention, let's talk about calcium." He chortled, pleased with his perceived cleverness.

I knocked on the door of the doctor responsible for the medical students.

"Hi, Ruth, come on in. What can I do for you today?"

"Well, sir, we had a lecture on calcium metabolism and the doctor showed pictures of naked women first."

The doctor chuckled. "And?"

"Well, sir, I don't think that's appropriate and it doesn't teach young doctors to have proper respect for women."

"Oh, come now. You're over-reacting. It was a joke, for heaven's sake. A joke. Was the lecture good?"

"Well, yes, it was, after he got down to chemistry and not naked women."

"Well, if you're learning about calcium, forget about the rest."

"But, sir, I don't want to forget about it. It's not right."

"Ruth, I suggest you do forget about it or else start thinking about a new career." He picked up some papers. The discussion was over.

I left that room exasperated.

This was only the first month of medical school and already I was coming home almost every day with tears of frustration rolling down my cheeks. How could I ever imagine then that coming home to cry after a demoralizing day at the hospital would continue almost daily for the next five years.

Now, Sophie, you might be asking yourself why I didn't just let it go. Truthfully, I was not as offended by the photos as I was offended that this school that I thought would be respectful of everyone was just the same as all the rest of the schools run by men.

I would be encouraging sexism had I said nothing. To laugh or to sit in silence is to be complicit with "the boys." I hope you feel confident enough to speak up every time you encounter sexism or racism or anything else of which you don't approve. To sit in silence, or smile at the "joke" is allowing sexist or racist people free rein to think it is okay to be like that. It is not okay. And only when strong women and men challenge the others will things change.

Sometimes when we want something so badly, we just have to grit our teeth and put the time and effort in to get whatever it is. I am not saying it is easy, but I am saying it is worth it. Going through medical school was difficult. Don't get me wrong. I love learning, and I love everything about medicine. It was everything else that was proving difficult. For example, hearing sexist comments almost daily was wearing and oppressive. I worked very hard and obtained very good grades. But I was often at odds with prevailing sexism and my good grades did not protect me from several threats of expulsion. So the lesson here is this: if you want something badly enough, don't be afraid to fight for it with every fibre of your being. I guarantee you it will be worth it in the end.

I was standing by my desk, shaking my head.

"What's wrong?" Dr. Satland asked.

"Oh, I keep asking the guys to take down all these photos of naked women, and they refuse. It's disrespectful to women, and since we are supposed to be a new breed of doctors, a different kind of physician, it disturbs me that we are encouraging them to do that."

"Well, of course they refuse. Boys will be boys, after all. This is just what we expect from our medical students."

"You expect them to treat women with disrespect and to sexualize half the population?"

"Look, Ruth, if you can't handle it, perhaps you should just drop out right now. This is only the beginning. You can always quit medicine, you know."

"Oh, I can handle it, sir."

"Well, I suggest you start figuring out how to fit in and stop complaining about these insignificant matters."

I sat down wearily and thought, I can handle it all right. And no matter what he says, these are *not* insignificant matters! That night I went home again with tears of frustration in my eyes.

I guess I did not help matters much by my next move. I went to New York for a quick visit with my old roommates. While there, I made a purchase that I kept hidden in my drawer at school. I waited for the right moment. It came soon.

There were frequent tours through our medical school, often in an effort to raise money for the medical school building still under construction.

One day, a tour of about fifty people emerged from the elevator. Dr. Satland was walking to greet them. Just before he passed me, I quickly taped up my New York purchase over my desk as he approached. When he saw the four-foot square photo of a naked guy with his schlang hanging down past his knee, he ran up to me yelling, "What are you doing? Take that down at once! What if they see this?" His face was red, little balls of spittle forming at his mouth. He was so furious he could barely talk as he looked at the extra-large poster of the naked man, then looked at the fifty people approaching us.

"Take that down. Now," he hissed.

"But, sir, I'm only trying to fit in, as you suggested."

He tried to say something, but only more spit showed up on his lips, accented by his reddening cheeks.

I turned to my naked guy. "If you don't like it, I guess I can take my poster down . . . but only if the guys take theirs down too. It's only fair. Do ya'think?"

"Fine. Take it down. Take them all down. But do it at once," he shouted, leaving to meet the nice people wanting to tour our progressive school.

"Well, fair is fair," I said to him as he was leaving. "I'll take mine down, and they will take theirs down. I don't mind fitting in that way."

He turned back, his face scarlet with anger and frustration. "Take. That. Down. At. Once."

Thank goodness—I couldn't stand to look at it one second longer.

That is why there were no more pin-ups hanging up in our area and also why I got a reputation as a "ball-breaking bitch," whatever that might actually mean. Things were never the same after that. Dr. Satland made things as difficult and unpleasant for me as he possibly could for the rest of my time in medical school and during my residency. But I never regretted putting up that poster.

ON MONDAY, OCTOBER 5th, I walked into class, distraught that Janis Joplin had died the day before, presumably from an overdose. I had always admired her, and I loved her music, playing it full blast in my little orange Fiat convertible sports car with quadraphonic sound. (I finally had my sports car, trading in the Buick for the Fiat after I started medical school; my father was so happy I was in medical school he didn't even mind that I now drove a "foreign car.")

"What's up, luv?" Ron asked. "You're not looking too chipper today."

"I'm just sad about Janis Joplin. You know, she was my hero."

Howard looked up from his desk. "Oh, you mean your her-o-in." He chuckled at his macabre wit. I did not think it was funny at all. It seemed no one ever took me seriously.

Our medical training started at Foothills hospital. Since this was a newish hospital and since we were the very first medical class, there were no clinical clerks or residents above us. Just us and 102 doctors, all professors at the new medical school and all eager to impart their knowledge to the students. I think we all knew what a phenomenal opportunity this was and we revelled in being the darlings of the hospital.

There were only two women on staff at Foothills: Dr. Tess Trueman, a gynaecologist and brilliant surgeon, and Dr. Barbara Rostrum, a family physician. I wondered what it was like for these two, being the only women. I knew there was a doctors' lounge, and that there was only one bathroom for males. There was a male doctors' changing area on the surgical floor, with separate change rooms for the orderlies. Women physicians who needed to change into scrubs had to do it in the nurses' change area. None of the men seemed to think this was remotely significant and the few times I mentioned it, I was ridiculed.

I had hoped that Dr. Rostrum would become a mentor for me but I am afraid I screwed this up myself.

Because we medical students were so few, and there were so many doctors on staff, it was not unusual for us to spend afternoons learning in doctors' offices from the very beginning of our training. In the second month of medical school, I found myself in the offices of Dr. Rostrum. She was a good family physician, with a solid reputation, and I hoped to learn a lot from her. Dr. Rostrum asked me to interview patients, take a history, and then report back to her. However, late in the afternoon, she made an exception.

"This next patient is one that I will see alone. You are welcome to sit here and wait for us." She left the room to see the patient and, shortly thereafter, they both returned to the office where I was thumbing through a medical book. Dr. Rostrum introduced us and walked around to her desk. I looked up at an elderly woman. She had on a dark grey dress, lisle stockings, black oxford shoes, and a small, blue hat. She also had a very large stomach. In fact, she looked as though she could be nine months pregnant. But she also looked to be in her eighties.

Dr. Rostrum spent a few minutes setting up a follow-up appointment with her, and then the patient very slowly got up and left the room.

"What do you reckon is wrong with her?" Dr. Rostrum asked.

To this day, I am ashamed and mortified by my answer.

"Pseudocyesis?" I glibly replied, proud that I knew about false pregnancies so early in my training and anxious to be done for the day.

Dr. Rostrum looked at me with pure disgust on her face and slammed her book shut.

"That's a terminal cancer, a large tumor. She does not have very long to live. I think that's enough for the day. Go home."

I did not know what to say or do. I immediately realized how completely inappropriate and unfeeling I had been.

"I'm sorry," I stammered, "I didn't know . . ."

"Just go home, Ruth. That's enough for now." She turned to her papers.

I could never blame her for not becoming my mentor or for disliking me because it was my own damn fault for being so arrogant and unfeeling. If there was any consolation prize for my behaviour, it would be that I learned a powerful lesson about sensitivity and caring for patients and those people around them, and hopefully never made such an ignorant error again.

That day I learned a lesson that might help you too, Sophie: never put a clever quip ahead of sensitivity for another living being.

"HEY, RUTH, GUESS what?"

"What?" Ron and I were walking towards the staff lounge on the eighth floor of the hospital. It was eight-thirty p.m. and I was going to sit down for a few minutes before returning to my studying.

"Garvey is operating tonight. Well, he's doing the anaesthetic. He's going to meet some of us in the lounge and take us into the OR. Are you in?"

"Really? Really scrub?" Ron was used to hospitals. He had been a head nurse for the past seven years. I was interested but didn't want to faint again like I had watching plastic surgery slides.

"C'mon. It will be a blast."

"Okay, I'm in." I smiled. I was kind of excited actually.

We walked into the lounge. Howard was there with several others from the class.

"What's in there?" Ron asked Howard, indicating an IV bag on a stand that he was wheeling around.

"The usual," Howard answered.

"Welcome to the big time." Ron put his arm around me. "Have a drink."

First, he squirted some "IV fluid" into his mouth, and then held the tube by my mouth, waiting for my lips to open.

"Wait. What's that?" I asked.

"Vodka," he replied and took another squirt.

I opened my mouth and received a big blast of booze.

Just then Dr. Garvey walked in.

"Hey, gang, how are we all doing? Get over here, Howard."

Then he took a long squirt of vodka.

"Are we all ready to go down to the OR?" He looked around the room.

"Aye aye, sir," we answered.

Before leaving to change, I pulled Ron aside.

"Ron, I'm confused. We're going into the OR, right? With a real patient. Why are we drinking vodka? You know I'm not a prude, but this is pretty dangerous, isn't it?"

"Nah." He put his arm around me. "We all just had a little, just for fun. It's not dangerous. C'mon, let's get changed."

There was a door off the lounge that led down the stairs directly to the OR suite. I went into the nurses' lounge to change and met the guys in front of the OR. I kept thinking how unacceptable this was, and how we shouldn't be drinking vodka. Or any alcohol, for that matter. I loved drinking, but under these circumstances, it was just wrong.

I felt confused by the whole situation as Ron stood beside me and instructed me how to properly scrub. This was not pretend. It was real. There was a real live human being on that operating table. I couldn't believe that every one of us had vodka in our bellies. Hopefully, the surgeon did not.

"Hi, Joe," Dr. Garvey bellowed out to the surgeon. "Brought some helpers along with me tonight."

"Fine. Just keep 'em all on your side."

Dr. Garvey put the patient to sleep, quietly explaining what he was doing. Then he motioned me over with his finger.

"Here, Ruth, you start this IV in his arm. We'll need a second IV for some of the drugs."

I looked up at him. It's a good thing I had the surgical mask on because my mouth was wide open.

"Dr. Garvey, I've never done anything like that before."

"Right, and there's always a first time. Here, take this. I'll show you what to do."

And so with Dr. Garvey whispering in my ear, I started my first IV on a living person who lay unconscious on an operating table. I was in my second month of medical school.

Many years later, I learned that Dr. Garvey had left the hospital and gone into treatment. Apparently, someone opened his locker to reveal many hundreds of pills and vials of drugs. Ron told me he was rarely sober. But, I never did hear of his causing injury to a patient. To his credit, after his own rehab, he opened up a rehab hospital specifically for doctors who had become addicted and was very successful in his new career. I always liked him and hoped he didn't suffer too much, although I suspect someone taking the amount of drugs he was purported to take was likely sufficiently tormented.

Recalling that incident, I realized how conflicted I had been. On the one hand, I wanted to be part of the group and be one of the regular medical students for a change. On the other hand, what we were doing was just wrong. It really was unacceptable and I felt very confused. I loved drinking, but under these circumstances we were not approaching this surgery with the seriousness that we should have had—I mean, we were going down to operate on a human being! However, I was part of the group, accepted as one of them, all going into the OR. I am ashamed to say how easily I succumbed to peer pressure. If the group was drinking vodka, then I would too. I thought a lot about it afterwards and was truly ashamed both by my behaviour and by my fear of challenging them.

Sophie, I truly hope that you learn how not to give in to peer pressure. At times, it can be a powerful thing. Do what is right for you, what feels good. Listen to your insides and follow your instincts. Sometimes we choose to believe that which is easy to believe, like a few sips of vodka before surgery is harmless. Things are not always as they seem, and we need to make up our own minds even if it goes against everyone else.

IN THE FOURTH month of medical school, I became very fatigued, something that was quite out of character for me. As a medical student, naturally I was going to diagnose myself, which I did. I decided I had mononucleosis and I called my doctor to tell him that. Of course he did not believe me. A first year medical student, a woman no less, was telling him what her diagnosis might be. That was an affront to him. He became very indignant at my having the temerity to tell him what was wrong with me but he agreed to see me and run some tests.

After much blood work, x-rays, physical exams, and more, he came to the conclusion that I had mononucleosis and that I needed to stay home for a while.

"How long is a while? I can't miss any classes. No, I absolutely can't stay home."

"Well, Ruth, your liver is very enlarged, your glands are huge, your blood work is very abnormal, and you are contagious. You have to stay home until it is safe, not only for you, but for the rest of the students. Let's monitor you closely, but I think it might be a couple of months."

"A couple of months? No. That's outrageous. I worked too hard to get into medical school. I can't even miss one day, much less any longer. I'll just go to school and be very careful."

"Tough break. Maybe they will send your work home for you to do." Dr. Vigenstrod looked at his watch, stood up, and put his hand on the door.

As the tears started falling, he softened a little but remained his authoritarian doctor self.

"Look, I know your professors and I will tell them you have mono. You are *not* to go back to school under any circumstances until you are better. Do you understand that, young lady?"

Young lady, my ass, I thought. He's not the one in medical school.

"Look, Doctor, please, I'll rest a lot, really, but how about if I just go to some lectures . . ."

"You'll do nothing of the kind. Go home. Go to bed. Get your blood checked every week. Come here every two weeks for a check on your liver and spleen. And do not, I repeat, do not go back to school until I say so. Do you understand?"

I couldn't understand why he was being so mean about it. He wasn't the one missing out on lectures.

Now the tears really did come fast and furious. I wasn't able to wait until I got home first.

When I called Dr. McArthur, a pediatrician and one of my favourite student advisors, and told him the news, I said it looked like I was going to miss the exam on the cardiovascular system.

"Don't worry, Ruth," he reassured me. "We'll help you out. You can write the exams when you are ready."

Many, but not all, of the professors were supportive and said I could just pick up when I came back to classes.

EVERY MORNING AT ten o'clock, while lying on my bed, I went to Sesame Street, where the Count taught me fun ways to get from one to ten, and Big Bird taught me a new way to say the alphabet.

Ron started dropping over every day to bring me up to date on what we were learning in classes. Mostly I would lie on the bed in my pink fuzzy robe as depressed as I had ever been.

"Ab-keh-defghi," I mumbled.

"What's that, luv?"

"It's the alphabet, Ron. Big Bird is teaching me the alphabet."

"Ruth, are you feeling okay? I mean, really?"

"Yeah, I guess so. I'm just supposed to lie here, so I thought I'd learn the alphabet the way Big Bird says it. "Ab-keh-defghi . . .""

"What on earth are you saying?" Ron asked.

"Look, Ron, if you write the whole alphabet out in one long line, like ABCDE etcetera, and then you read it, you get ab-keh-defghi-jickle-manoprah-stuvwysizz. You know, as opposed to saying A, B, C. Ab-keh-defghi—"

"All right, I get it, I get it." He smiled. "Look, these are the notes from today's class . . ."

So, while my fellow classmates were studying the cardiovascular system and learning about myocarditis, I was lying in bed with Big Bird for company, trying very hard not to develop it.

AFTER TWO MONTHS, Dr. Vigenstrod gave the okay for me to return to my classes. I had missed almost the entire cardiovascular system and exam. And I was worried.

The exam had been a big one—it had taken all day, with many and varied slides and exhibits to define, multiple choice questions, identification of anatomical parts and more. When I felt I was ready, I notified the appropriate professor who told me I could sit the make-up exam at one p.m. the following day.

However, when the time came, Dr. McGregor walked in and handed me a small piece of paper. At the top of the paper two words were written:

"Define shock." That was it. No slides, no exhibits, no multiple choice, no identification of significant body parts exposed in cadavers, just, "Define shock," which is what I was going into looking at that paper.

"Well, okay," I thought, "I will give this a good shot." I took a deep breath and started writing. I wrote for hours, bringing in all the different parts of shock, anatomy, physiology, causes, treatment, and so on. After writing for three hours, I turned it in and thought that it was pretty good, considering. The examiner's face turned into an ominous grimace as he took the exam from me, which should have been my first clue.

The next day, I was called into the office of the dean.

Sitting there with him was Dr. McGregor, the one who administered my "exam," and Dr. Satland, sitting there with a huge smirk on his face. He seemed to be everywhere I was.

"Ruth," the dean started, a sad smile on his face, "you failed your cardiovascular exam. I'm sorry but you will have to leave medical school."

I almost fell off my chair.

Once I sat up and regained my composure slightly, I asked, "How do you know I failed?"

Dr. McGregor answered, "You were given an exam, you wrote it, I marked it, you failed."

"Did you even bother to read my exam?" I asked.

"Of course I read your exam," Dr. McGregor barked.

"But I was the only medical student who ever wrote that exam. How do you know how other first year medical students would do? What are you using as a reference? What did you compare it to? This was absolutely nothing like the exam the other students wrote."

I looked from him to the Dean.

"She has a point there, Mark." The dean frowned.

I jumped at this. "You can't kick me out of school for being the only medical student in the whole world who ever took this exam. You have nothing to compare it with. It's just not fair. But if you kick me out, I will go to the press and tell them what you did. We all know this has nothing to do with the cardiovascular system." I was dredging up all the indignity I could muster.

I took a deep breath. 'You did this on purpose. I know you do not want me here." I stared at Dr. Satland. "But I am not going to go quietly. I want a rewrite, but a fair rewrite, not a set-up. This is what I propose—I would like to take the cardiovascular exam with the second class coming in, when they take it next year. Then my results can be judged against other first year students. If I fail, I will leave quietly, but if I pass, I will continue. If you don't let me do that, I will make sure what you did to me is made public and will be in every paper across Canada."

All three men looked distinctly unhappy.

Now, Sophie, this was the very first time I made such a threat, but certainly not the last time. I had no way of knowing that this was just the beginning. I loved my medical school, and I wanted it to be as good as possible. I knew some professors, especially Dr. Satland, were still angry at me over the Playboy pin-up debacle and they tried to get me out of the school in as easy and quickly a way as possible. It didn't work. So another lesson, Sophie, is this: fight for what you want. Being scared doesn't mean you don't have the courage to do things. Always stay true to yourself. When you don't know how you will ever find that courage, dig deep inside yourself, find what you need, and fight on. Fight for yourself, for what you want, for women all over the world, for what you believe in, for the benefit of what you are working on, but fight fairly and intelligently.

By the time we all left the dean's office, it was agreed that I would continue on with my classes, and that I would take the Cardiovascular System Exam the following year with the next class. If I failed that, I would be kicked out of school; if I passed, I would continue with my class. Of course, by now Dr. Satland was even angrier with me as were the professors who had set the new "exam" for me. Truthfully, I think they were all a little ashamed at their obvious effort to oust that "feminist bitch."

However, the dean tried to support me as much as he could although he had to listen to his professors. But not everyone complained about me. The Heads of Paediatrics, Immunology, and Gastroenterology all seemed to like me, and I excelled in their courses. They were very encouraging and supportive. But most of the other doctors tried to make things uncomfortable for me when they could, hoping that I would drop out.

I kept asking myself why I was such an unpopular student with many of the other doctors. When I thought about it, I realized I was disliked mostly by the older, more rigid doctors, while many of the younger doctors liked me just fine. I was known as a feminist, which for some was a bad word. Why, I never could figure out, since it only meant equality for women and men. Women in those days were supposed to be subservient, something that did not come naturally to me. I never would have gotten into medical school by being subordinate to men. I felt that my ideas and opinions should be just as valued as anyone else's.

As it happened, I was also the only Jewish student in the class but by no means the only one at the school. Several of the doctors were Jewish and, although I would like to think the fact that I was Jewish was insignificant, I'm not completely sure that was true.

Also, I fought back. If something seemed wrong to me, I said so. Doctors like Satland did not approve of that at all. I was seriously trying to be part of a wonderful new entity, the University of Calgary Medical School, First Class, and was very proud to be there. But that didn't mean I had to accept every single thing just because a doctor said it. That attitude was not appreciated.

When I was in high school, I used to love to write stories. Some of them I thought were actually pretty good. But Mrs. McQuarrie, my high school English teacher, did not. I remember two short stories in particular I wrote when I was in Grade Ten. The first was actually a paragraph. The topic of my paragraph was war, and I wrote the whole thing in incomplete, short sentences, because I thought that when it was read, it sounded like a machine gun. It did too.

But not to Mrs. McQuarrie. I got an F. She told me if I ever became a famous author, I could use incomplete sentences, but as long as I was in her class, I had to use complete sentences.

The second short story was about a young girl who had been a passenger in a car which was involved in a very bad accident. The girl was now lying mangled at the side of the road. She was the narrator of the story and described the scene until everything slowly went black.

Mrs. McQuarrie did not understand my story. Even when I explained that everything went black because the girl died, she still did not get it. I got it though—an F is what I got.

For many years after Grade Ten English, I thought I was a terrible writer, and didn't know anything. Even though something deep inside me told me that both of those stories were better than a grade of F, I still could not show anybody anything I wrote.

By the time I reached medical school, I had already figured out not to automatically believe what others tell me. Listen to them, yes. Listen hard, consider it, and then decide for myself if the person is making sense or not. For me. Mrs. McQuarrie was not logical. Dr. McGregor was not logical. Dr. Satland was not logical. For me.

The lesson here, Sophie, is to get as much information as you can from other people, but do what feels right for you. If something feels wrong, or out of place, examine it very carefully. Believe yourself. Believe *in* yourself. There will always be down times. There always are, inevitably, in everyone's life, but even in the midst of a down time, your essence is still there somewhere. Maybe depression or inertia is covering it up, but it is there. Find it. Trust your native goodness.

WE STARTED WORKING very early on in our first year at the free clinic downtown. I loved the free clinic—I've always liked working with young people. We would take blood samples, do interviews and help the on-call doctor. One night, I stayed late to help out and was asked by the doctor to deliver the blood and other specimens to the lab at the hospital. I left the clinic just after midnight, and by the time I delivered all the lab specimens to the hospital, it was well after one a.m. We had a lecture the following morning at eight a.m. followed by a two-hour break. I decided to stay at the hospital overnight in an on-call room, go to the morning lecture, and then go home for a shower and change of clothes before afternoon classes.

At eight a.m. the next morning, I was at my desk, cup of coffee in my hands, looking forward to the morning's lecture. In walked Dr. Satland with two doctors behind him. He walked to the front of the room and looked around.

"Simkin. Out!" he yelled.

"I beg your pardon, sir, what?"

I was completely taken aback by this.

"Get out. Go home. No female student of mine is coming to classes in jeans."

"I'm sorry, sir, but I worked at the free clinic last night, and we're encouraged to wear jeans there. I had to bring the lab specimens to the hospital, so it was late when I was finished and I decided to stay here overnight. And we're not seeing any patients this morning, so I thought . . ."

"I don't care what you thought or what kind of excuses you are making. No woman will sit in this class in blue jeans. Go home and put a dress on before you come back here. Now get out!"

Usually I managed to hold the tears off until I got home and closed the door. This time, they almost betrayed me. I walked past Peter, sitting with a sad smile, eyes looking down at his sandals and bare feet. I guess that was considered appropriate dress for the men.

Now, Sophie, this really happened, less than fifty years ago. When I look around now, and see women physicians dressed for comfort, it doesn't seem real that women had to wear skirts or dresses just to sit in a room for a lecture. This was the way of the world and, if I wanted to stay in medical school, I had to play by the rules whether I liked them or not. It's amazing when I remember that in the 1940s and 1950s, when the Western World finally authorized the existence of a women's ball team, the women were not allowed to get off their tour buses unless they were wearing clean skirts. That's the way it was. I'm sure that most, if not all of the players would rather have been in slacks. But, if they weren't in skirts, they were heavily fined and they really couldn't afford that with their measly salaries of $45.00 to $85.00 for the entire season. Things have not really improved in this area.

Sometimes you have to play by rules with which you don't agree. I could think of worse things. The lesson here, Sophie, is to pick your fights. Fight for change constructively. Pick your issues carefully. No matter how much you push the envelope, it will always still be stationery. So make sure your issues are worth your energy. Don't let trivial matters get in your way. Wearing dresses to hear Satland pontificate? It's stupid but who really cares? Wearing mini skirts in ICU or ER? Definitely worth the fight.

"Simkin, clean off that board!" Satland yelled at me one day while we were waiting for a lecture to begin. Why he usually picked me to do the housekeeping when there was a room full of others, I don't know. But he did. I knew, as I was erasing old material from the blackboard, that he was making faces and signs at me behind my back. I could hear some tittering from the room. If he felt he had to act like an idiot child, I guess that was his prerogative.

Day after day, Dr. Satland and the others would try to discourage me from staying and, if they couldn't do that, then they would at least make my time there as miserable as possible. Everyone noticed it but no one wanted to "make waves" or in other ways stand up for me. I know that most everyone was pretty sure I would never graduate, with everything that was put in my way by Dr Satland and associates. I thought differently. If I had to survive by coming home every night and crying, so be it. Mostly I tried to laugh. Damn fools, thinking they could make me quit just because things were difficult. They didn't know me at all.

I DIDN'T ALWAYS feel that I had supporters, but I did. I had the friends I met through Laurie, and they were supportive, although none of them really knew what medical school was like. Joanne could imagine, but she hadn't started med school yet. And then I met Muriel.

Muriel had always been active in the community and ultimately became the Chancellor of the University of Calgary. Her husband was a well-known and accomplished dentist and hypnotist, who also taught at the medical school.

One day, Muriel got a phone call from one of the doctors.

"Muriel, we'd like you to do something for us. We have a first year student here, a young woman who doesn't know many people in Calgary. Her language is atrocious—she swears like a drunken sailor—and her behaviour is not always appropriate. We wondered if you might consider taking her under your wing a bit. She needs all the help she can get."

"Well, sure, Don, we can try. What's her name?"

"Her name is Ruth. Ruth Simkin. She's a Jewish girl. I hope you can help her out a bit."

So I got a phone call from a stranger who invited me over to her home for Shabbat dinner the following Friday night and that is how I came to be friends with Muriel and Dave and their three children. I did not know about the phone call to Muriel until many decades later. All I knew was that a very nice woman invited me over for Friday night dinner. I missed my family terribly, especially Friday night dinners when we ate together, so I jumped at the chance to have a family encounter, even if it wasn't my own family. Muriel's two sons were about my age and her daughter slightly younger. We all became friends. One of her sons was my lawyer for the entire time I lived in Calgary.

My language—well, that is another story. As is common in places like long-term hospitals, prisons, and other institutions, the "inmates" develop a highly specialized language that is not always appreciated in standard society. That's exactly what happened to me. I had become so used to swearing when I was in the hospital, that I had trouble returning to "civilized" language.

Muriel is a very elegant, distinguished woman and, over time, maybe a tiny bit of that rubbed off on me. I certainly did not feel comfortable talking in my usual institutionalized manner when I was in her presence. Today, we are closer than ever, seeing each other as often as possible. She has been a constant stabilizing factor in my life. Sophie, the lesson here is to try to learn from other people who have a different way of being, even though it is not what you may be used to. It can truly enrich your life and improve your options for how to exist in the world.

I was lucky in that it has always seemed easy for me to commit myself. In our first year of classes, a doctor presented a patient to us. He described all her symptoms and what her life was like, talking for quite a while. Then he asked if anyone could figure out what was wrong with her.

I put my hand up. "She has Systemic Lupus Erythematosus."

"You can't say that," the doctor yelled.

"Why not? Doesn't she have Systemic Lupus Erythematosus?"

"Well, you haven't ordered any tests at all. What do you base that on?"

"I base it all on what you've told us."

"Well, you can't do that. You have to order tests first."

"Oh, okay." I sighed. "First I would do . . ." and I went into a lengthy list of tests I would order and with each one, the doctor gave me the result. After I had gone through all the appropriate tests, I tried again.

"Based on the results of all the tests, the patient has Systemic Lupus Erythematosus."

"*Now* you can say that," the doctor exclaimed, a touch of annoyance in his voice.

Truthfully, I would rather rely on my gut, although of course it's critical to know all the information from the tests as well.

I've always felt that women were more instinctive and intuitive and men relied more on hard analytical data. Neither way is better or bad; they are just different. But I don't think that the doctor should have dismissed my initial diagnosis so quickly; I suppose he could have asked me how I came to that conclusion. I believe it's an asset to be able to make the diagnosis using hard data in combination with intuition, although I was alone in my thinking.

1971-1972
Second Year of Medical School

EARLY IN MY second year, we were sitting in a seminar given by Dr. Keith Pearce, the head of psychiatry. He paced up and down across the front of the room, his hands gesticulating. He was tall, over six feet, and took long strides. His brown hair was combed over to the side and occasionally fell over his forehead. He was solidly built, not fat, but he looked like an inflexible truck.

I had always been interested in psychiatry and toyed with the idea of doing a residency in it. Dr. Pearce quoted some studies which somehow didn't sound right to me. I actually looked them up after the seminar and checked a few other things he mentioned. Dr. Pearce had been making things up. There were no such studies as the ones he quoted. I mentioned this to Ron who had worked at the hospital for years before medical school.

"He can do whatever he wants, Ruth."

"But, Ron, he lied. He just made things up."

"Doesn't matter. Nothing will happen because everyone is scared of him."

"Scared of him. Why?"

"Well, he has a lot of power around here. He doesn't hesitate to hurt people."

"I don't get it. The guy is head of psychiatry. He's involved with the med school. He's on all these committees. If he's such a bad guy, why don't they just get rid of him?"

"I told you already. Everyone, and I mean everyone, is scared of him."

"Well, I'm not scared of him."

"You should be. He can do you some serious damage."

Shortly after that, we were to observe a family therapy session. I sat with Ron and several other students behind the one-way mirror, watching a husband and wife interviewed by a psychiatry fellow and staff psychiatrist.

The psychiatrist turned to the woman. "What exactly are you doing, dear, that is upsetting your husband so much that he feels he needs to hit you?"

I was shocked. I could not believe what I was hearing. Both the staff psychiatrist and the fellow kept asking the woman questions like that, implying it was her fault that her husband was an abuser. We watched the woman sit there sobbing as the blame was piled upon her, while the husband sat tall in his chair, legs spread open in front of him, arms hooked over the back of his chair, a smirk on his face. I wanted to rush into the room and tell her they were all wrong, that it was not her fault at all. Ron, who knew me very well by then, grabbed my arm and sat with me saying softly, "Let it go, luv, just let it go."

A third incident followed shortly after that calamitous family therapy occurrence which was the final nail in the Ruth-might-do-a-psychiatry-residency coffin. I was working on the psychiatry floor and was asked to come into a room. Once I was there, a patient on a gurney was wheeled in. There was a small table beside the gurney with ECT (Electro-convulsive Therapy) equipment on it.

The psychiatrist in the room looked at me and said, "I would like you to administer shock treatment to this patient."

"No." I just looked up at him. "I won't do it."

"Dr. Simkin"—they called us "doctor" when we were on the wards and in white—"please administer shock therapy to this patient at once."

"No. Absolutely not." And I turned to the patient and said, "You should not be having shock treatment. There are other ways for you to get better."

Then I walked out of the room, heart pounding, but I felt I had no choice. I could not be complicit in giving someone shock treatment. I had seen what shock treatment could do to people and getting better was not usually the end result. That incident got me in a bit of trouble too but, more importantly, it made me realize there was no way I could ever survive a psychiatry residency.

DURING THIS TIME in medical school, I lived with Joanne, whom we called Joey. She also applied to medical school, got accepted, and would be in the year behind me. I loved living with her and looking at her—her freckled face, her blonde-red hair, her smile, her quietness—quite the opposite of me. We got along well. She worked as a respiratory therapist at the hospital. Lungs were my weak point. I was good at immunology and gastroenterology and we helped each other a lot.

Joey was a softball player, playing with a team that hoped to make it to the Canadian finals that year.

"Come to practice with me tonight, Ruth. After practice, we're all going to go out."

"Oh, I don't know, Joey. I gotta study."

"You always have to study. Just come one night. You've never seen me play or met anyone else on the team. We're good, you know."

"I'm sure you are. Can I read if I go?"

"Sure. Take a book with you. You can sit alone in the stands too, if you like."

"Okay, sure, I'll come. Let's go play ball!" I gave her a hug and received a big one back.

Off we went to the ball park where Joey and her team were practicing. Her coach was Joanie, former all-star player whose reputation as a great coach was never far away. I watched a bit but was aware of the heavy book in my lap and all the information in it I didn't yet know, so mostly I sat there high in the stands and read.

I happened to glance down at the field at one point and there were a group of women around Joey and Joanie, with someone else pointing up at me. I turned my head and waved my right arm. The woman waved back. Then I went back to my book.

Joey later told me that the coach came up to her and asked who that person was with her head in a book. The players were fascinated that a person could come to the ball park and read. This was not in their frame of reference at all. So before I even met any of them, I was already known as being very different. I was "The Doc" from that day forth. After that night, I went with Joey more often, and pretty soon I found myself in their dugout, being the team doctor. I wasn't a doctor yet, but they loved the idea of having a team doctor. I enjoyed sitting in the dugout reading and, when needed, bandaging up knees and arms and giving the odd injection. I even accompanied them to the Canadian Finals as their team doctor.

Joanie, the coach, and I became close friends from that very first night until she died of lung cancer almost fifty years later. Her death left a huge void in my life.

Y'know, Sophie, one never knows where we will meet people who become important to us. I could never have guessed that going to the ball park that night would provide me with the opportunity to meet my best friend for almost half a century. Always be open to who and what is around you. You might discover some very pleasant surprises.

ONCE JOEY BEGAN first year, we had fewer parties since we both had to study more.

I remember one Saturday night, when pretty much everyone I knew who wasn't in medical school was going to a big party, and I was sitting at my desk, gnawing on broiled chicken necks, my food of choice when studying. One plate could last me for many hours. I sat back in my chair, looking up at the ceiling.

"Am I insane?" I asked the wooden beams above me. "Everyone I know is at this party, and here I am, Saturday night, sitting at home with a plate of chicken necks. I have to be nuts." I picked up the sign I had on my desk that asked, "Is there life after med school?" "Is there?" I asked it. "I sure hope so, because I'm doing this thing. I am going to be a doctor, no matter what it takes, party or no party." I put the sign down, cracked open a new book, and began to read.

"Our cardiovascular exam is coming up," Joey mentioned one day.

"Oh, when is it exactly? I'm supposed to take it with you."

"Didn't they tell you?"

"No. I haven't heard anything. When is it?"

"It's next week, Thursday."

"Thanks, Joey. I'll check in with the dean. Maybe they were hoping I would forget and then they could try to kick me out again. But you know, I think I'd better disguise my handwriting and do everything I can so the markers won't know it's my exam."

"That's a great idea. I hear it's going to be similar to the one your class took last year."

"Great. I am so ready."

A week Thursday came and I wrote the exam along with the other fifty-four students in Joey's class. I was very careful to disguise my writing and was delighted to see that all the exams just had numbers on them, no names, so I felt fairly hopeful that the markers wouldn't know my exam from anyone else's. I was confident that I knew the material. And I was right: I got the second highest mark. I'm sure Dr. Satland tried to figure out which paper was mine and maybe some poor student got a lower mark because he thought it might be my paper. I don't know. I was just happy to have done so well.

I WAS SITTING in the cafeteria with Dr. Trueman who had taken a few of us under her wings. She had become a mentor, teaching some of the most important lessons I learned in medical school.

"Don't ever be afraid to declare yourself," she said one day. "Even if you are wrong, you must say what you believe and why." We were having a rare coffee in the cafeteria. Dr. Trueman worked harder and longer than anyone else I had met so far.

She leaned over and whispered confidentially, "You see that group of doctors over there." She indicated with a quick nod of her head, covered with striking, steel grey shortly cut hair.

I looked over to see four doctors sitting at another table.

"When they make a differential diagnosis, they might have twenty diseases on the list. They think that listing that many diseases makes them look clever. But they are wrong. They are just too ignorant to narrow down the list to a more appropriate few. You never need to have twenty items on a differential diagnosis. Two or three is enough if you know your stuff. Don't ever be afraid to say what you believe."

I nodded. I knew some of the students did the same thing. When we were supposed to figure out a diagnosis, they would go on and on listing things, when the diagnosis was obvious. At least, obvious to me. I thought if I could be half as good a doctor as Dr. Trueman was, I would be in good shape.

"When I first came to work here some years ago," she continued, "I had already completed extra fellowship training. I applied for hospital privileges but, probably because I was a woman, they wouldn't give them to me."

"Get outta here! Why? You had all that extra training."

She nodded. "I did. But they didn't know me. They said I could have partial privileges if another gynaecologist on staff corroborated everything I did. For a while."

"You can't be serious."

"Oh, I am. And this went on for a few months. Every time I saw a patient in emergency and wanted to do surgery, one of the other gynaecologists had to come and check out my diagnosis."

"Weren't you upset by that?"

"Sure I was. But it didn't last for too long."

"Why not?"

"One day a young woman came into emergency and I examined her. I could feel that she had an ectopic pregnancy; it was tiny, the size of a small pea, no bigger. I wanted to operate right away."

"Wow." I loved these stories and could listen to her forever.

"Carlos came down to check my diagnosis."

"Carlos! Get outta here, no. You're a much better doctor than he is."

She smiled and shrugged. "Well, he couldn't feel the ectopic. And I said I wanted to take the young woman to surgery immediately. You know, if she doesn't have surgery quickly, the ectopic could rupture, and she could possibly die, or at least become seriously ill."

"So?" I asked, wanting more.

"Well, because I wanted to take her to surgery and Carlos couldn't feel the ectopic, he called Bernie."

"Bernie?" Both Bernie and Carlos were gynaecologists on staff.

"Yes, Bernie. And he couldn't feel it either. I felt badly for the young woman, because she was uncomfortable and she had to have all these extra exams. But she was my patient, and I knew what I felt, and insisted that I take her to the operating room. But because the other two could not feel it at all, they told me that if I took her to the OR, and was wrong, I would lose what little privileges I did have in the hospital."

"Nothing like putting a bit of pressure on you." I shook my head in amazement. Dr. Trueman was an excellent doctor and to have her judgement questioned just didn't seem possible.

"I took her to the OR, and both Carlos and Bernie scrubbed in with me and, of course, there was the ectopic, smaller than this." She held her thumb and first finger almost together to indicate how tiny it was.

"After that, they left me alone and I didn't have them looking over my shoulders checking up on me all the time."

"Gosh, it should have been you checking up on them, not the opposite."

She smiled. "Just be sure of yourself and confident, not afraid to speak out for what you believe to be true. Don't ever be afraid to commit yourself."

That was good advice, Sophie, and it has stood me in good stead for almost fifty years. Hopefully it will be a good lesson for you too: Don't ever be afraid to commit yourself, to stand firmly for what you believe to be right.

WE WERE ENCOURAGED to think of our patients as "whole people," not just parts of a system, and therefore psychology and sociology were included in our courses. This was one of the reasons why I loved my medical school so much—it made eminent sense to me. We even had an obligatory half-hour teaching on homosexuality; that's actually the word that was used—nobody said "gay" or "lesbian" in those days—we were all homo-sex-uals. It was a ridiculous teaching session, not only because it was taught by heterosexuals who may or may not have known lesbians or gay men, but the information presented was not particularly accurate. After this half-hour of so-called education, one of the guys in class stood up, quite perplexed.

Gary looked around and said, "You know, if I could only meet a *real* homosexual, a real live one, I might be able to understand them a little."

I would have liked to have said this out loud but I really did want to graduate, so instead I thought to myself: Gary, you damn fool. You've been hanging out with one for the past few years, you have several teachers who are gay men and lesbians and you see us every day. You just don't know it, which is the point; we are not that different than you at all. Just regular people.

It was a difficult decision for me to make, not to come out when I was in school. But I already had enough problems and being an out lesbian would have been the end for me, of that I am certain. I did become completely open the day I left my training.

I remember an incident many years after Gary's outburst. I had a friend who taught social work at Mount Royal College. She asked me if I would come talk to her class about lesbians. I agreed and gave my little presentation. One of the women in the room, who appeared a bit shocked that a lesbian was in the same room as she was, asked, "But what do you all do when you get together? I mean, what do you actually *do?*"

"Well," I smiled at her, "when my friends and I get together, we usually drink tea."

I'm sure she was expecting some X-rated descriptions but I was being truthful. We usually did drink tea.

OUR SOCIOLOGY PROFESSOR, Dr. Larson, had a very good idea. There was a course for young couples about to be married, sponsored by the Catholic Family Service Group. It covered numerous topics over ten evenings. One day, Dr. Larson handed out random assignments. Steve and I were to attend the course that very week. We were not sure what the topic was, but I didn't care—I was sure to find it interesting. Our assignment was to write a critique of that part of the course.

Steve and I walked into the crowded room of an elementary school where fifteen young couples sat at desks that were a little too small for them. All of them were engaged and planned to be married within the year. We squeezed into desks at the back of the room and settled in to observe. There were rows of letters from the alphabet lining the wall all around the room. Too bad Big Bird isn't here, I thought, smiling, remembering Ab-keh-defghi. A large easel was set up in front of the blackboard.

A man and a woman walked in.

"How do you do," the man addressed the room. "My name is Dr. LeBlanc and this is my wife Maureen. We are here to talk to you tonight about sex for young married couples."

I sat up, interested to hear what they would say about honeymoon cystitis, premature ejaculation, and other matters that young newly married couples

need to know. And also, I admit to being slightly wary at the introductions—
Dr. LeBlanc and Maureen. I heard it all the time and wished I didn't. Did he
really consider these differing forms of address to be equal? Steve and I lifted
our eyebrows and looked at each other. A murmur filled the room. At least
now we were sure it would not be a boring evening. We were wrong.

Dr. LeBlanc straightened his pale blue tie. His white shirt and blue suit were
impeccable, with very sharp creases in the legs. His dark curly hair was oiled
and combed. Some might think he was good looking. I was not one of them,
although I had to admit his appearance was pretty perfect. Unfortunately, I
could not say that about his thinking and his presentation.

Dr. LeBlanc put a chart up on the easel. It was a large graph, with pink
and blue lines. To my utter amazement, he began discussing the differences
in diastolic and systolic blood pressure during orgasm of men (blue lines) and
women (pink lines).

"Is this a joke?" I leaned over to Steve. I couldn't believe what I was hearing.

"I don't think so," Steve answered. "I think he's serious."

Dr. LeBlanc spoke on and on about blood pressure and orgasm to a room
of totally blank faces. The young people had absolutely no idea what he was
talking about.

When he had exhausted the pink and blue lines lecture, he then sat on the
edge of the desk and held out his hand. Maureen, in a pink print shirtwaist
dress, high heels, clutching a purse with her bright red fingernails, came over
and took his extended hand.

Dr. LeBlanc again addressed the group. "Maureen, my wife, and I get
along very well. We never fight. That is because I remember to bring her
flowers several times a week."

"And," Maureen smiled, "I always have dinner on the table and make sure
I have a pretty negligee to wear each night. These things are important to
preserve the harmony of the household."

Dr. LeBlanc and Maureen looked like a perfect couple. They were stylishly
dressed and smiled at each other and us a lot. However, what came out of their
mouths were vacant words, full of nothing.

"Oh look, Steve," I learned over to whisper, "they match their orgasm
chart. So cute."

The majority of faces in the group were blank. Not mine though—I was
irate. I stayed until the end of the talk. There were no questions from the

group, even though Dr. LeBlanc and Maureen had encouraged the group to interact. The young people looked as though they could hardly wait to get out of that room. Never did the two lecturers mention any of the problems two virginal people would come across in the first days of marriage and newfound sexuality.

"What a shame," I said to Steve as we walked down the hall towards our cars. "This could have been such an important lecture for all of them. What are you going to say in your report?"

Steve shrugged gloomily.

I drove home and started writing.

Three days later I was called into the dean's office. Dr. Larson was there, sitting in a chair across from the dean's desk, and Dr. Satland, who always seemed to be around when I was in trouble.

The dean was holding a piece of paper in his hand which looked very much like my sociology report. "Can you explain this?"

"I don't understand, sir. Explain what?"

"What exactly is this? What are you trying to do?"

"I was writing a report of a class we attended as we were instructed to do, sir. Is there a problem?"

"Is there a problem?" Dr. Satland mimicked angrily.

The dean read from my report:

At no time during this class were these youngsters informed of any kinds of sexual problems that might affect young newly married people. Pre-mature ejaculation, honeymoon cystitis, foreplay, sexual variations, all important aspects of a pre-marriage class, were studiously ignored. As well, the class was given unreliable information regarding the presentation of flowers and the wearing of sexy negligees, in lieu of any real data. As a new medical school in this city, it is our obligation to censor this group and to close down these classes or, barring that, to offer to teach them ourselves, so that these young people can get information that would be relevant to their new start in a married union. Not to do so would be irresponsible and a very poor showing for this medical school. Action must be taken at once so that future classes can get information that will prevent problems, not take classes that will cause them.

"And I suppose," the dean asked, "that you think you are going to take on the Catholic Church?"

"Well, no actually, Dean. I had hoped you would."

I was, indeed, serious. I was furious that my school, the school I thought was respectful and responsible, would have anything to do with such courses. I had truly believed that we were supposed to write a report that took into account what we heard and present an analytical review of what we had observed. It really did seem to me that these young pre-marital couples were not only being treated unfairly, but also irresponsibly by the medical profession, and I was in a position to help them out.

The dean, Dr. Larson, and Dr. Satland did not think so. They were livid.

The dean wanted me to apologize to pretty much everyone for writing such a report. I didn't think I had done anything wrong and apologizing seemed silly. Words were spoken and voices were raised. It was suggested that I leave the school. Again. I refused. Again.

"We are asking you," the dean fluttered the paper in my face, "to forget about this whole incident."

"But, sir, what about the classes? What about all the kids who don't get the information they need? Don't we have a responsibility as a medical school to . . ."

"Shut up!" Dr. Satland bellowed. "Dean, we need to drop our losses now. Let's just kick her out before she embarrasses us any further."

"But, sir, I'm only trying to help . . ."

"Your help, as you call it, can only cause embarrassment to the school. We have to work with the Catholic Church and the courses they offer. Don't you see the trouble that your report will cause?"

"But don't you understand how we are being irresponsible?"

"You cannot save the world, Miss Simkin, as much as we all know you would like to." Dr. Satland placed his hands on his knees. "I think we should ask Miss Simkin to leave medical school right now."

I felt the tears in my eyes. I really did want to help. I didn't mean to cause any trouble. I sat down heavily in the chair across from the desk, trying very hard not to let my tears show.

The dean tore up my report. He threw the small pieces into the garbage can under his desk. Remember, Sophie, this was in the days prior to computers and there were no other copies at all.

"We will forget about this incident. There will be no more reports from you. Go back to your classes and do what you are told. You are not to go out on any more assignments like this outside of the medical school. Do you understand?"

I nodded, stood up slowly, and walked out of the room, a room with a silence so loud I thought my head would explode.

1972-1973
Third Year of Medical School

MY LAST YEAR had arrived and I was still in medical school. We had turned the corner into 1973. All things being equal, it would be the year I would graduate. You may ask yourself why I went through all the trouble, and dealt with so much pain and aggravation, especially from those who did not want me there. If everything was such a struggle—why do it? I would sometimes ask myself the same question. Because it was totally worth it, I would answer, even with all the tears and hassles. Absolutely. I never regretted anything except my own arrogance and stupidity. I was still here and it looked as though I might actually make it. It seemed the requests for me to leave were becoming half-hearted now. I always fought back. I always threatened to call in the press, and I always stayed in school.

I knew that many of the professors felt they made a mistake by accepting me, but I also knew that there were more than a few who realized that I was going to be a good physician and those doctors stood solidly behind me. Nevertheless, I felt opposition from certain professors to the last day of medical school and into my residency. I always knew the dean supported me but he also had to listen to the other professors. I felt pretty certain he was one of the doctors who was delighted that I actually graduated.

Three weeks before our graduation, I got called into the dean's office.

The dean sat behind his desk, Dr. Satland paced the room. Dr. McGregor sat, hands on thighs, looking down at the floor.

"Well, Ruth," the dean started, "it looks like graduation is coming up soon."

I stood in front of the dean's desk, not having a clue what I had supposedly done, curious as to what was coming next.

"It looks as though you will be graduating with your class," the dean said.

I smiled, tentatively. He didn't call me into his office to tell me I would graduate with my class.

"I have something here," he pulled a paper out of a pile on his desk, "that I would like you to sign."

"What is it?" I asked.

"Oh, nothing really important," he said. "It's just a statement saying that you were not asked to leave medical school. That you will be graduating."

"Not ever asked to leave?" I smiled at him.

"Well, you know, it's just routine. Just sign here." He held the sheet across the desk while the others looked on.

"Gee, Dean," I picked up the paper, "I accept your apology for asking me to leave medical school, but there is no way I am signing anything. At all."

"Ruth, it's just routine. Go ahead and sign it. Be done with it and you graduate in three weeks," Dr. Satland said.

"Are you telling me that if I don't sign this I won't graduate?"

"Oh no, no, not at all." The dean was looking distinctly uncomfortable.

"Look, thank you for everything. Really. But I am not signing this paper. Or any other like it. Other students aren't being asked to sign papers like this, are they?"

"You should have become a lawyer, not a doctor," Satland mumbled.

"Can I leave now?" I asked.

The three men looked at each other before the dean nodded at me. I got the feeling he was asked to do this by the other doctors who were afraid of future legal problems because I had threatened to sue them and to go to the press. However, the dean apparently did not agree with my signing any papers. Both he and I were relieved when I left without signing anything. I always felt he supported me but was under pressure from doctors like Satland who were always trying to kick me out of school.

I walked out of the dean's office and, three weeks later, attended my graduation where I received my Doctor of Medicine degree.

I'VE HAD GRADUATIONS in the past, but none like my graduation from medical school. My parents and siblings were there, several sets of aunts and uncles from all over North America, my former therapist, Dr. Brennecke, who would never have missed this event after having saved my life less than ten years previously. The new medical school building officially opened at this graduation, and that was where we all stood to take the Oath of Hippocrates.

I meant that Oath as I stood and repeated it with the other graduates. I felt good, dressed in a black and white silk blouse under a black jumper with a flared skirt. I was Dr. Simkin. I was now an MD, Dr. Satland notwithstanding. I still had to get through my residency, but I felt that would be small potatoes compared to the struggles of the previous years. I was a doctor and no one could take that away from me.

The new medical school was beautiful, but I was pleased and honoured to have been a graduate from the top floor of the hospital in make-shift rooms, the first medical class of the University of Calgary. Standing there with my friends, saying the Hippocratic Oath together—well, it was as if I were in a dream. But it was real. I really was a doctor. I looked forward to the residency that would be starting imminently.

"What's that?"

"It's called a Wild Mustang, my favourite celebratory drink," I answered my mother, as we were all out for yet another festive dinner. "It's vodka and champagne, and I love it. Want one?"

My mother took a small taste, smiled, and went back to her wine.

"Mom, can you believe this? Can you believe I really am a doctor?"

"Yes, dear, I can. We are so proud of you and we love you very much." She put her arms around me and gave me a big hug. You know, all those years of coming home from medical school upset and hurt was worth that one hug. Sophie, I'm so sorry you didn't know your great-grandmother. She was a wonderful woman and my biggest supporter.

Things were good. I was now a doctor, and my family was with me. I had decided on a Family Practice residency. I loved the idea of being a doctor to a family for years and years, delivering children and then the children's children. I had a firm idea of what it took to be a good family doctor, incorporating the art of healing alongside the science. I felt pretty confident about the art part; I just needed to learn more of the science.

Recently, my friend Rob sent me a newspaper article that appeared at that time. The headline was, "First Class of MDs Graduate at U of C." There were three of us, myself, Mike, and Gord, who had decided upon Family

Practice residencies. The rest were all going to specialize in other areas. The article names the three of us by our first and last names, and mentions that twenty-six of us have recently graduated with MDs. It then went on to refer to me, not once, but several times, as "Miss Simkin" while describing that I had become an MD. It seemed as though the reporter simply could not address a young woman as Dr. Simkin and had to stay with Miss Simkin, MD notwithstanding. The men were never called "Mr." but were referred to by their full name. Even though the article was about the Family Practice Residency based out of the Ambulatory Care Centre, "Miss Simkin" kept jumping out of the paper and everything about the residencies stayed in the background for me. Here I was, an official doctor, being written about as a new MD, and still being referred to as Miss Simkin as though it were impossible for the journalist to see me as a doctor alongside all the male doctors.

Truthfully, Sophie, at times I am weary that my mind immediately goes to these minutiae. These small matters are critical to why women are not in a position of equality in the world. And I will unfortunately keep seeing things like this when I read newspapers, internet articles, anything at all, that does not completely keep women and men equal in words, in meaning, in intent, in feeling. I hope, when you see these things, that you don't let them slip by. With each slip, we lose valuable ground. Moving forward demands of us that we do not let these small matters slip. Otherwise, we will be so much worse off than we are now.

1973-1974
First Year of Residency

"HI. MY NAME is Marlene. I'm Dr. Saunders' nurse."

Marlene Conrad was a beautiful woman with long, bright red fingernails, classy jet black hair, but it was her smile that entered my heart and stayed there.

"Dr. Saunders, the head of the Family Practice Department, will be your preceptor during your two-year residency in Family Practice."

"Okay. How come?" I asked.

"Well." Marlene seemed to hesitate, then smiled sadly at me. "Usually the doctors argue over who gets the *good* students. Everyone argued over you, but it was different. No one wanted to work with you, so they decided to hold a lottery. Dr. Saunders lost, or he thinks he lost. I think he's wrong." She grinned. "I watched you on the wards last year. I know you are a really good doctor. He'll find out soon enough. And because I'm his nurse, I'm yours now too."

I grinned back at her. "Well, I guess that's good for me too, Marlene. Thank you for being honest. That's important to me. I appreciate it. You can help me figure out the lay of the land here, okay?"

From that day on, the two of us became fast friends, drawing closer all the time. We worked together for the next seventeen years, and she always made things easier and a lot more fun. Without question, Marlene made me feel much better after the pain of learning about the lottery to see who would "get" me. That's still hurtful forty-five years later.

Although I chose to specialize in Family Medicine, I still did the normal rotations throughout all the departments in the hospital. I spent several months each working in internal medicine, surgery, pediatrics, gynecology, and so on.

My first rotation at the hospital was internal medicine. On my second day, Mr. Davis died. He was an eighty-nine-year-old male who had been comatose the previous day when I met all the patients for whom I was responsible on the ward. I had to notify the family.

His daughter arrived on the unit with her husband and daughter.

"Mrs. Sampson, I'm so sorry to tell you that your father has died." I felt the tears run down my face. After all, it was my first real "death."

"There, there, dear." Mrs. Sampson put her arm around my shoulders. "Is there someplace calm we can go?"

I nodded and we walked down the hall to the quiet room.

"You realize this is not a surprise for us, we were expecting it," she gently explained. I nodded. "Don't feel badly, dear, I know all you doctors did everything you could for him. He was an old man. We all have to go sometime."

I nodded again. "I'm so sorry."

"There was nothing more you could do, dear."

And so, Sophie, my very first "real patient death" ended up with the patient's family consoling me, instead of vice versa. I felt a little foolish but I have never really been ashamed to show my feelings.

The second week, when I was on call at night, I was sitting at the nursing station writing in the charts when a nurse came to me.

"Mrs. Stewart isn't breathing well," she said.

I knew that Mrs. Stewart was a woman in her eighties who was unconscious after a stroke. She had a breathing tube inserted which was supposed to help her breathe better. I went to see her and, sure enough, she was struggling to breathe and had started to turn blue.

I immediately called the doctor in charge, who explained that he had been talking with the family, that they didn't expect her to survive, and so I should just pull the tube and let her die.

I asked the nurse to return to the room with me and said, "Pull the tube, please."

"I'm not pulling that tube. You pull it."

"Well, I'm not pulling it either," I answered. I didn't want to be the one causing Mrs. Stewart's death.

We both left the room and went back to the nurses' desk. After several unsuccessful attempts at trying to get someone else to pull the tube, I finally realized that, if I was going to be a doctor, this was my responsibility and I simply had to go into her room and do it. I was not happy to be responsible for a death a mere ten days after I started being a real doctor, especially since Mr. Davis, my first patient, had just died a few days earlier.

I went into the room, undid the little white cotton strings holding the breathing tube in place, took a deep breath and pulled the tube. Almost immediately, she was breathing easier and started to pink up. Apparently, that breathing tube was blocking her breathing, not helping her at all. Once it was out, she was able to breathe normally.

Two weeks later, Mrs. Stewart walked out of the hospital. I didn't kill her after all, and I learned a much valued lesson, which is also a good lesson for you too, Sophie: not everything goes the way we think it will go, or should go. We need to be prepared for any outcome and always be open to the unexpected.

"RUTH, HAVE YOU worked at the Belcher yet?"

"What? I don't know what you mean." It was my second week of residency and I did not understand what Carolyn was asking. She was one of the senior residents, hired from another medical school so we, the first class of residents, would have more experienced residents working with us from whom we could learn.

"It's a great set-up. I was just there last night. They pay you two hundred bucks for the night, and you go there to be on call. I never got called once. I studied all evening, slept all night, and got paid two hundred smackeroos for it. You should try it."

This sounded good to me, so the following week, I presented myself to the head nurse at the Colonel Belcher Hospital for veterans, as the resident who would be on night call. She showed me to my room but, since she was very busy, said I should discover the hospital by myself. I thanked her and settled down at the small desk to study.

Not five minutes later, I got a call to go to emergency. There was a man, very drunk, who had fallen and bumped his head.

"C'mere, baby, I wanna feel your warm body against mine," he said, as he reached out and pulled me towards him. I pushed him off, but he kept grabbing at me.

"Hey girlee, c'mon, give us a kiss." He laughed.

I tried to examine him but he kept grabbing and poking me. I had to get two orderlies to hold him down while I examined him.

I dealt with him in about forty-five minutes and then went back to my room to study. Carolyn didn't tell me about having to do emergency visits, I muttered to myself, as I walked over to the desk. My bum didn't even hit the chair before the phone rang. At the same time, I heard overhead, "Code doctor red, code doctor red, Unit 3 South." That meant an emergency. Except I had no idea where Unit 3 South was. I ran out into the hall and continued running. I stopped the first person I saw. I was panting as I asked, "Where's Unit 3 South?" She pointed. I continued running.

I got there and was met by a nurse.

"Oh, thank goodness you're here, Doctor. Mr. Wilson coded."

I followed her to Mr. Wilson's bed. I saw a comatose, very skinny, elderly gentleman. One of the first things to do when trying to resuscitate a person is to give them some IV meds that might help them regain consciousness or at least breathe more easily.

"Let's start an IV," I said.

"We tried to," the nurse answered. "We couldn't start it."

"Well, let me try."

I put the tourniquet on and looked. No veins. Poor Mr. Wilson's veins were all collapsing.

"Well, I'll have to do a cut-down. Please bring me a cut-down tray."

"Right away, Doctor."

Now, Sophie, that sounded pretty good, didn't it? "Please bring me a cut-down tray." In fact, that was the right thing to do, to start a cut-down. But the truth of the matter was that, although I knew about cut-downs and had read about them, I had never even seen one done before. A cut-down is an emergency procedure when you don't have veins available and need one immediately, so you cut open the patient's arm (or groin), expose the vein, and put the IV in that way. Now, theoretically, I was the one in charge here, right? So I had to act the part.

"Here it is, doctor, the cut-down tray."

"Thank you," I answered, as I put on my sterile gloves and mask.

After I was done and we had a good IV running, when Mr. Wilson was breathing normally and looked okay for an unconscious guy, I turned to the six nurses and orderlies around the bed. "Thank you all for your patience. That was really the first cut-down I've ever seen."

"Well, you did it very well," one of the orderlies replied.

I spent the entire night by Mr. Wilson's bedside, ordering different fluids and cardiac medicines. I had to call Joanne at home a couple of times to ask her what to do next and to have her look up some things for me, but I whispered into the phone and don't think they knew I was doing that. Thank goodness Joey was the heart and lungs expert in our household.

Just before seven a.m., I sat down and said, "I think we're good now. The EKG seems okay, his breathing is okay, his colour is good. I think I'll go back to my room."

Just then, a man walked up to Mr. Wilson's bed.

"What's this?" he shouted and started fiddling with the IVs that I had worked so carefully to adjust in the first place.

"Who is that?" I asked the nurse.

"That's Dr. Strand. He is Mr. Wilson's doctor."

I walked over to the bedside. "Hello, Doctor. I am Dr. Simkin, the resident on call."

"Are you the one responsible for this catastrophe?" he yelled.

"I'm not sure what you mean."

"Look," he said, as he pulled out the IV, "this old guy is on his way out. You don't need to save this old alkie. You residents, really." Within minutes of Dr. Strand's ministrations, Mr. Wilson's monitor was showing a flat line. Of course. He had stopped everything I had done. And he let Mr. Wilson die.

"These old guys don't need all this stuff," he yelled at me and stomped off.

I went back to my room, gathered my stuff, drove to Foothills Hospital and started work on the ward at eight a.m., less than an hour after Mr. Wilson died.

I didn't go back to the Belcher Hospital much after that. Carolyn may have had good experiences there but mine were not so good.

TODAY MY HANDS are all gnarled and seriously deformed from the arthritis which has taken over my bones and joints. I wasn't always like this, I used to be quite skillful with them. For some reason, I seemed to be particularly talented at starting IVs. I often could "get them in" when others couldn't. A twenty-three year old woman with leukemia, Wendy, was on our medical ward and needed lots of IVs. She was not expected to live. When I was on the internal medicine rotation, it was part of my job to start her IVs but, after I left and went on to other rotations, I often got calls from other residents or nurses.

"Ruth, can you please start Wendy's IV?" I started her IVs for all the months she was in hospital.

I was also comfortable talking to people who were terminally ill, so Wendy and I talked a lot. Very often, when I finished my rounds at night, I would poke my head into her room and, if she was still awake, as was usually the case, we would talk for hours. After I left internal medicine and went on to other rotations, I still went to Wendy's room to talk.

"Hi, Wendy. Can't sleep?"

"I'm worried about Duke." I sat down. Duke was Wendy's husband.

"Worried how? What's the problem?"

"We've only been married a few years. And now I'm going to be leaving him soon."

I took her hand. There was no use contradicting her. She would probably die within the next few months.

"What if he just stays home? What if he doesn't find someone else?"

"Y'know, Wendy, Duke is a smart guy. He'll take care of himself. Of course he will be upset. That's normal. And it's normal to worry about him. But there will be lots of people in his life."

"You're right, Ruth, I know that, but still, I can't help but feel I'm deserting him, ya'know?"

I nodded. We sat in silence in the middle of the night, holding hands, each of us thinking hard on what life brings to people.

When we had two weeks off, Rob and I went to Mexico together. While I was there, I bought a little onyx egg for Wendy. I thought she might like the feel of it; it was something she could hold onto in bed. When I came back and went to her room to give her the gift, someone else was in her bed.

"Where's Wendy?" I asked the nurse at the nursing station.

"Oh, Ruth, I guess you haven't heard. She died last week."

And you know, Sophie, almost fifty years later, that little onyx egg sits on my window sill. I see it every morning when I wake up. Some people, like Wendy, are very unlucky, and some people, like us, who are living, are very lucky. I never want to forget to be grateful, every day, for the life I have. And,

Sophie, it's a good idea, every morning when you wake up, to take just a few minutes to realize how lucky you are and how much you have. And offer thanks for that to whomever you might believe in. If you don't believe in anything or anyone, then offer thanks to the universe. And think about how perhaps you can help others who are not in such a good situation. Our lives are so fragile, just like a real egg. We must be careful with the lives we live and those of others.

"SO, SIMKIN, I hear you want to go on a luxury cruise."

A smiling Dr. Satland addressed me thusly in a very crowded elevator, encouraging the others to laugh at me with him. I had just applied to do an elective on a Hope Ship, a hospital ship that went to war-torn countries and offered medical assistance to those who were severely in need. It was anything but luxurious. It would have been hard work under difficult, uncomfortable, and dangerous circumstances, and something I hoped might lead me to work eventually with Medecins Sans Frontières (Doctors Without Borders). Each resident got to pick a three month elective as part of our residency, and I wanted something challenging and away from Calgary.

I wasn't surprised when I heard my request to work on the ship had been denied. I heard it was Dr. Satland who had vetoed it. Whether or not he thought it truly was a "luxury trip" or he knew what it was and didn't want me to have the distinction of doing something like that, I'll never know. I suspect it was the latter though. I had to pick an elective much less exciting. But as long as I was still in this hospital and learning, dealing with Satland was just another medical training challenge for me. It was difficult, but I would get through it.

Not long after I started seeing patients in the Department of Family Medicine, I was summoned by Marlene.

"He wants you to see a patient," Marlene informed me. "She's in the room with the one-way mirror. Dr. Saunders brought in a group of doctors and students with him to watch. He says he's going to surprise you, to teach you a lesson, although I'm not sure what kind of lesson he had in mind." Marlene leaned over and whispered, "The patient is deaf."

"Thanks, Marlene. Appreciate it." I walked into the room with a teenager and an older woman. The teenager sat with her head down, arms on her lap, curly brown hair falling over her face.

"Hello, I am Dr. Simkin."

The older woman looked tired. "This is my daughter, Ella. She is deaf." She touched Ella's arm and her daughter looked up.

I signed. "Hi, Ella, how are you today?"

Ella sat up and brightly signed back.

I pulled up a chair and the two of us had a very animated conversation using ASL (American Sign Language). When the appointment was over, we agreed to meet again in a few weeks and I walked smiling out of the room.

I saw Marlene come out of the observation room. She could hardly keep a straight face. The two of us went into another examining room and closed the door. Marlene burst into laughter.

"I wish you could have seen his face. When you first walked into the room, he said to everyone, 'Watch this. That patient is deaf and Simkin doesn't know it.' The other doctors all laughed. They were all sitting on the edge of their chairs waiting for you to do something silly. But when you started talking with the patient using sign language, they all sat there with their mouths hanging open. I didn't know you could sign. And for sure Dr. Saunders didn't. Was he ever surprised!"

"There's a lot about me people don't know." I grinned. "But thanks for the tip-off. It helped a lot."

"I don't know why these doctors are always trying to trick you, Ruth, but you always outsmart them. You would think they'd give up already."

"They will never give up, Marlene. I just have to finish this residency, open up my own office, and be done with the lot of them. And then maybe you could come be my nurse."

"Maybe I could."

AFTER FINISHING MY internal medicine rotation, I moved on to surgery. I was assigned to work with Dr. Cruse, a South African surgeon on staff. On my first day, I reported for duty, anxious to learn some surgery.

"Hello, Ruth," he greeted me with a smile, "I understand you speak Greek. I look forward to learning some of it from you."

"Sure, Dr. Cruse," I smiled back, "and I look forward to learning some surgery from you."

He gave me a weird look, but then said, "Let's get started. I'll meet you in the OR in ten minutes. We're doing an appendectomy then."

"Great," I replied. An appendectomy, that's something that every family physician should know how to do.

Soon, I was in the OR, all scrubbed and waiting with Dr. Cruse while the anaesthetist put the patient to sleep.

Once Dr. Cruse could go ahead, he started with me, "Okay, Ruth, start teaching me Greek."

"Sure, Dr. Cruse," I replied, "but can you please explain what you are doing?"

"Don't be silly, Ruth. You're a girl. You don't need to know what I am doing. Just hold that retractor steady for all my surgeries, teach me Greek, and we'll do just fine."

"Dr. Cruse," I started tentatively, "I'm here to learn surgery."

"Not from me, you're not. Girls don't need to know any surgery at all. Just hold that retractor steady."

I finished out the surgery with him, holding the retractor since I was the only other doctor in the OR with him other than the anaesthetist, but I did not teach him any Greek. We worked in silence. When we were done, I changed and went to the office of the Head of Surgery.

"Dr. McPhedran, I really want to learn surgery. Dr. Cruse says he won't teach me because I am a woman, well, he says girl. He just wants me to teach him Greek, which I really wouldn't mind doing, if he would just teach me some surgery."

Because the men all changed together in the doctors' lounge, by the time Dr. McPhedran went around to talk to other surgeons, no one would work with me. Dr. Cruse had told them all—well, I don't know what he told them—but they all said they didn't want me on their team.

Dr. McPhedran called me into his office. He told me no one would work with me. I didn't know what to do. Frankly, I was puzzled, because I was serious about medicine, learned quickly, loved being a resident, and yet no one wanted to work with me.

"Leave it with me, Ruth. I'll see what I can do."

Finally, Dr. Mydland, who had a chief surgical resident, Dr. Preshaw, agreed to take me. I had always liked Dr. Mydland. He seemed kind and gentle and he had a good sense of humour. I decided I'd best not talk at all, just shut up and learn as much as I could. I didn't want to antagonize the last surgeon who would take me on.

They were both great. Dr. Preshaw taught me how to do an appendectomy, and I did some on my own. I learned a bit about pre- and post-surgical care, and some new surgical techniques. I worked hard, spoke little, and learned as much as I could.

Whenever Dr. Cruse saw me in the hospital, he sneered. If I had known how to sneer, I would have sneered back.

AFTER MY SURGICAL rotation, I went to the Intensive Care Unit (ICU). I was the first female resident to ever complete that rotation as part of a residency. Previously, some had tried, but hadn't made it for the full three months.

I loved working as a resident. The women residents, few in numbers compared to the men, all had to wear a uniform that I hated: a white jacket over a white blouse and white mini-skirt. And the mini-skirt was very much mini. In my surgery rotation, I had been in scrubs most of the time, even when doing my rounds. But now, in ICU, I wasn't supposed to be in scrubs.

I knew those white mini-skirts were a disaster the first time I led a cardiac arrest response. Usually, the ICU resident was in charge of codes in the hospital. A code is when a person's heart stops, a cardiac arrest, which could happen for a number of reasons, anywhere in the hospital. When a code was called, the ICU team came running with the nearest crash cart, while the ICU resident shouted orders, ordering medications, directing the team, and using the paddles to restart the heart and so on. Hopefully, within seconds or minutes, the patient's heart was restarted and the patient would then be transferred to intensive care. These codes were serious and physically demanding on the medical team. I was terrified of codes, but I wanted to learn how to do them.

My very first week in ICU, a patient's heart stopped while he was being transferred to ICU. I happened to be right there. I was only five-foot-four and those gurneys were high, so I hopped up on the gurney in order to do cardiac massage; the guy was almost dead, there was no time to waste. I didn't want him to die, so I straddled him and was working diligently, massaging his heart and shouting out orders. When I turned my head, I saw about twenty people, orderlies, nurses, residents, all standing behind me looking at parts of me that I wasn't interested in sharing. Codes were not the place for silly outfits like mini-skirts. After that first time, I tried to wear scrubs as often as possible, even though they preferred that we women wore scrubs that were dresses and not pants scrubs. But, running around a hospital, kneeling on the floor, or hopping up on a gurney to help someone while wearing a miniskirt or even a longer dress scrub, is not the best thing if one is reasonably modest. These days when I am in a hospital, I'm glad to see all the women physicians who are dressed in clothes that allow them to comfortably do the work they are supposed to do. In others words, they wear the same clothes as the men. I wonder if they are aware that women who preceded them by less than half a century could not dress like they do?

Y'know, Sophie, my mother, your great grandmother, wouldn't even let me go out for dinner with my family if I had on pants—clean, washed pants, mind you—I had refused to put on a dress because it did not make sense to me. I watched my parents, sister, and brothers all walk out the door, leaving me at home alone. I just couldn't do something I thought was silly and stupid—putting on a dress for no particular reason—and chose to stay home, miserable and hungry, instead of enjoying myself with my family having dinner over at a friend's home. When I think back, it seems that one of the things that bothered me the most about dress codes is that there was one set of rules for men and one for women. And the set of rules for women seemed to play into what men wanted women to look like, regardless of whether or not our clothes were comfortable and functional.

As I walked around the hospital in my scrubs or my whites, I would think of my uniform and smile at how much I loved the medical uniforms compared to the other "uniforms" I could have had. While I'm not partial to any uniforms, my medical ones were better than others with which life could have dressed me.

Both my grandmothers got up in the mornings and put on their uniforms, their aprons, and then they spent most of the day cooking. They both seemed to like this job and we always came to the kitchen to visit with them. My mother didn't wear an apron quite as much. She didn't seem to like it as much as her mother or mother-in-law. Sophie, I was so different from all of them and, occasionally, I would wonder if that was a bad thing. I always came to the conclusion that it was not a bad thing at all. In fact, it was a good thing. Sophie, it's okay to be different from our mothers and grandmothers if we want to be. That is, it's okay if we're doing what is good for us. It's not bad to be different. I encourage you to live your life in a way that has deep meaning for you. And hopefully your "uniforms" will be perfect for whatever you choose to do.

The ICU rotation was difficult in the extreme. I got through it because of Dr. Sonny Belinki, the head of ICU, and Willie Fudge, the head nurse. Dr. Belinki had been one of my supporters when I was in medical school. He was an excellent cardiologist and a great teacher. I really enjoyed working with him. And Willie—well, imagine standing there being quizzed by doctors and hearing the correct answer magically sounding in your ear. I believe that every good doctor succeeds because of good, effective nurses. Willie always knew what to do, always willing to share her knowledge with the residents. I won't ever forget how much she helped me.

While Willie was helping me in ICU, Marlene was doing the same every time I went to the Family Practice Unit. Marlene made me look good. Just before I would walk into a room, Marlene would come up and whisper, "That's Ann in there. Married to Peter. Three kids, youngest one, Carl, broke his leg three weeks ago. Ann is having a recheck after taking antibiotics for a urinary infection."

I would then walk in, sit down across from the patient, smile and say, "Hi, Ann. How are you doing? Finished with the antibiotics? No more urinary problems? How's Carl's leg—cast okay? How's Peter and the other kids?" Ann would think I was wonderful. I would think Marlene was wonderful. Everyone benefited.

AFTER SUCCESSFULLY COMPLETING my ICU rotation, I went on to Obstetrics/Gynecology. I was really looking forward to that because Dr. Tess Trueman, my mentor, was a gynaecologist and also because Betty Flagler was Chief Resident. Betty and I met as soon as she returned to Calgary from her studies in Toronto, and quickly became friends.

Betty looked like a pixie. She was petite and slight with very short brown hair and a face full of freckles. She was in her thirties but looked half her age. Betty was in the last year of her OB/GYN residency, having been a resident for five years already. I was excited to work with her. Shortly after she arrived in Calgary, she asked if I would go apartment hunting with her. I was delighted to do so and we quickly found the right apartment. After all, she was to be the Chief Resident at Foothills Hospital, no small feat. Although her parents both lived in Calgary and were very proud of her, Betty definitely needed her own home. As she was getting ready to sign the lease, the landlady held out her hand to stop Betty from signing. We both looked questioningly at her.

"Does your mother know you are doing this, dear?" she asked.

I burst out laughing, but stopped quickly when I realized that Betty was mortified. She really did look like a teenager.

"This is Dr. Flagler," I said. "Her mother is very proud of her and is very happy that she is getting an apartment and I'm sure she will be a frequent guest here. Dr. Flagler is Chief Resident at Foothills Hospital."

"Oh, er, I'm um so sorry, Doctor. I just thought . . ."

"That's okay." Betty smiled gently and signed the lease.

The first day of my OB/GYN rotation, I was sauntering down the hall at five minutes to eight, smiling to myself. How I loved being a doctor.

A nurse saw me and called out, "Hurry. Go change. Mrs. Louie is delivering right now."

I changed quickly into scrubs and went into the room where Mrs. Louie, a Vietnamese woman, was in labour.

"Hello, Mrs. Louie." I smiled, belying the fact that I had never delivered a baby on my own.

"She doesn't speak any English, Ruth," Lorna, one of the nurses, said.

Just then, Betty came in. "Hi, Mrs. Louie." She smiled. Mrs. Louie smiled back because Betty was a familiar face.

"I talked to her husband last night, Ruth," Betty whispered to me, "and he told me how to say 'push' in her language. It kinda sounds like *Noh*. So we'll try it and see what happens."

Betty and I took our places at the foot of the table. Mrs. Louis' legs were up in stirrups and she was having a baby now, all right. Betty looked at Mrs. Louie through her knees and said, "*Noh*, Mrs. Louie, *noh*."

Mrs. Louie pushed.

"Good, Mrs. Louie. *Noh*," she continued.

Mrs. Louie pushed some more.

All the while, Betty is explaining to me what she is doing, putting in the freezing for the episiotomy, and so on.

"Look, Ruth, the head is crowning. Okay Mrs. Louie. No *noh*."

Mrs. Louie pushed harder.

"No, Mrs. Louie, no *noh*, no," Betty said a little louder and Mrs. Louie pushed even harder.

"Um, no *noh*, no. Stop pushing," Betty said even louder. Mrs. Louie pushed on.

"I don't suppose you asked Mr. Louis how to say 'stop'?" I asked.

Betty's eyes looking up at me over her mask told me to just keep quiet.

Mrs. Louis delivered a very healthy baby, but my first morning in obstetrics was spent learning how to repair the fourth degree tear Mrs. Louie had sustained by blasting that healthy baby out. Betty and I laughed about that for many decades after, all the while still feeling sorry for Mrs. Louie. But we weren't laughing so much that morning.

During the residency, we delivered many babies. We also worked on the gynecology wards. We completed histories and physical exams on new patients, prepared them for gynecological surgery, post-op care, and so on. One day, I admitted Mrs. Tashchenko to the ward. She was a woman in her sixties who had come in to have some polyps removed from her uterus. I took her history and found out that she was a farm wife who worked hard on the farm all her life. She had had her period every four weeks, bleeding steadily for three of them, for over thirty years before they finally stopped altogether. I couldn't imagine bleeding for twenty-one out of every twenty-eight days and still working on the farm every day,

"Didn't you talk to your doctor about that?" I asked. Bleeding that long would make a person very tired. Not to mention anemic.

"I did once," she said, "but he said was okay. So I leave it."

I thought this was a pretty incredible story, but no longer relevant, since she hadn't had a period now for over twenty years.

I was making rounds late the following day. She was in her bed, recovering from her surgery that morning.

"Hello, Mrs. Tashchenko, how are you doing today?"

"Fine, dear, but I wish I would have cords cut."

"Your cords cut. Why would you wish that?" By now I was well versed in patient medicalese, and knew she meant having her tubes tied.

"Well you know, dear," she looked a bit sheepish, "so I could be free."

"Free? What do you mean, Mrs. Tashchenko? Free how?"

"You know, dear." She paused. I didn't know. I looked at her, puzzled as to what she could mean.

"So I don't have babies, and then I could have sex."

"But Mrs. Tashchenko, you haven't had a period for over twenty years. What are you talking about?"

"Mrs. Pavlychko down the road have baby when she is sixty-one. Sixty-one. Yes."

A bit more questioning revealed that since Mrs. Pavlychko had had her baby, apparently at sixty-one, Mrs. Tashchenko thought she herself couldn't have sex until she was well beyond that age, without also becoming pregnant.

"No, no no, Mrs. Tashchenko, that's not how things work."

I went to the nursing station, got a big pad and pens and pencils and came back to Mrs. Tashchenko. I sat on the edge of her bed and, for almost an hour, I drew out the reproductive system, what it means to have a period, how people have babies, and why she couldn't have babies now.

When I was done, I said, "And so, Mrs. Tashchenko, you see, from what I've told you, can you now understand that you can't possibly get pregnant? You can safely have sex now if you like."

She looked at me and smiled. "T'ank you dear, I didn't know all dat before." She nodded. "But I still don't t'ink I take da chance."

Dr. Trueman had been trying to find something to prescribe for women who suffered from dysmenorrhea, very painful cramps with periods. Most women could deal with their periods easily, but some women had excruciating pain. It was possible their pain was exacerbated by other gynecological conditions, but for whatever reason, when they got their periods, they were unable to work, unable to do much of anything for three to five days a month. She decided to try NSAIDS, non-steroidal anti-inflammatories. This was in the days before anything for dysmenorrhea was available. She started prescribing Naproxyn with excellent results. With her encouragement, I started prescribing it for patients who had extremely painful periods. Soon, both of us were being ridiculed, mostly by the other gynecologists on staff.

"Oh look, here they come, the Naproxyn twins. Had any painful periods lately?" Carlos Casso was walking down the hall.

I looked at Dr. Trueman, my raised eyebrows a question.

"Carlos," she called out, "come on over and tell Dr. Simkin here what your opposition is to Naproxyn."

"Gladly, my dear." He leaned up against the wall, one soft desert boot up against it. "Everyone knows there is no such thing as painful periods. These women are just jerking you around. Maybe they want drugs. Maybe they want attention. But painful periods? Really? You really believe that?"

"And you don't?" I leaned up against the wall beside him. I took a deep breath and said, "Yes, I do believe. I have seen enough women now who complain about it so, yes, I do believe in painful periods and I believe that NSAIDS help them."

"Just because they complain about it doesn't mean they really have pain. You are just too gullible." And with a smirk, he pushed himself off the wall and continued on his way.

"He's wrong, isn't he?" I turned to Dr. Trueman.

"Yes, he is," she answered.

Five years later, dysmenorrhea had become a big thing, and one of the recommended therapies by the College of Obstetrics and Gynecology was exactly what Tess had taught me. I'm glad we stuck to our guns and were ultimately vindicated.

EVEN THOUGH I loved my little log cabin, I decided that when (for me it was never an "if") I graduated from medical school, I would rebuild and make it a bit larger. I was always having visitors and overnight guests and wanted more bedrooms and a slightly more modern bathroom and kitchen. With the help of my dad's construction company and my friendly architect, I designed what I thought would be the perfect home for the next few decades.

And looking back, I wouldn't have done anything differently. It did turn out to be perfect for me.

While my new home was being built, I was in my first year residency and living in a trailer on the edge of my property. The fact that I had four dogs and a cat made it a bit more crowded, but not quite as crowded as when Julia, the St. Bernard, had eleven puppies.

Let's back up a bit. In 1969, I spent some time travelling around the world. I thought I had best see some of the world before I settled down for my studies. At times I had a car and travelled with a couple of Australian friends.

One day, we were driving through the Swiss Alps and came to the Great St. Bernard Pass. As we were driving through, I stopped the car.

"Look, the Monastery of St. Bernard. Let's go look at the dogs."

In we went, telling the monks we were interested in seeing the St. Bernard dogs, which they were famous for breeding. In no time at all, I had bought one. I was told it would be several years before the dog would come to me, as she wasn't born yet. But I did get to pick her parents. And of course, I still had Jennifer the St. Bernard at home in Calgary waiting for me.

So, I started getting dogs from Switzerland. First came Stella, who actually turned out to be psychotic. You may never have heard of a psychotic St. Bernard, but Stella was for sure. After Stella left us—she had to go to doggie heaven when she became a danger to both humans and animals around her— Julia came. Julia was a beauty. Where I found time for this I don't know, but I started showing her in dog conformation trials, and she had her championship before she was even out of puppy class. She became quite well-known in the St. Bernard world and people asked after her pups. I had visions of making lots of money from her and her puppies. I started reading about the proper breeding of the dogs, and knew not try to breed her until the second heat at the earliest.

So when Julia's first heat came, I made sure that the dog run was as secure as possible. It was a very large dog run, so I wasn't worried about leaving them in it; they had a nice comfortable dog house, and so much room to run around amongst the trees and rocks and grass. They loved it.

"Whatever you do," I told the workmen who were building the new house, "do not, I mean not ever, let the dogs out of the dog run. Do you understand? Don't let them out at all." And then I went off to work, confident that Julia would remain in the dog run until I came home from work.

Silly me! I came home to find Julia running around the property with the German Shepherd from next door. Of course she got pregnant and all my great breeding plans were for naught.

I was then living in my trailer with a very pregnant Julia, and Peppy the poodle and Jennifer the St. Bernard and a cat and occasional humans. One day Julia started to deliver puppies. I had never seen puppies being born before and knew nothing about it. But as soon as I saw she was going to have her puppies, I did what any young doctor would do—I quickly drove to the hospital, ran up to the delivery room, got a bunch of cord clamps and other equipment used for deliveries, and hurried home.

By the time I came home with my cord clamps, she had already delivered one puppy and I waited for the others. She had ten more healthy pups, eleven in total, and never once needed my assistance or a cord clamp, all of which remained in the bag.

That was another lesson for me: Mother Nature knows what she is doing and doesn't need our help. The best we can do is observe and marvel at the exquisitely intricate and wonderful way she works. Julia knew what to do, even though it was her first litter. I was filled with wonder, but I didn't have much time to be fascinated since eleven hungry pups were now crawling all over Julia wanting to be fed. I had to figure out a system using pieces of scotch tape as there were eleven hungry mouths and eight teats. The poor little runt, Jonah, would never have gotten any milk if I hadn't given him a hand with that.

So there I was, living in a trailer with a friend, four dogs, a cat and eleven puppies. I was a resident, working every third night and week-end as well as very long days. The trailer was extremely crowded, but I was happy. I loved being a doctor more every day.

IN THE FIRST week of my pediatric rotation, I was in the office of the head of pediatrics, Dr. Gerry Holman, when he got a phone call.

"From the zoo you say?"

My ears perked up.

"How sick? How old is the baby?" Dr. Holman listened.

"When do you need the pediatrician?" he asked. Silence as he held the phone.

"Okay, we'll send someone out. But we don't have a lot of experience with orangutans. Okay. Thanks."

"Me. Please, pick me. Oh please, please puleeeease." I wasn't even sure what I was asking, but zoo, baby, and orangutan was quite enough information for me.

"They want a pediatrician at the zoo," Dr. Holman explained, "because they feel that the baby orangutan would be closer to a human infant than an adult ape. You really want to go?"

"Oh please, please, Dr. Holman, yes, I really, really want to go. May I?"

"Well, I have to send someone so I don't see why not. But please come back and tell me what you found and what you did."

"Oh thank you. Thank you. I'll go right away."

Dr. Holman smiled at me. It was so rare for something nice to happen to me those days in medical school and residency, that I just couldn't believe my good luck. And that is how I got to treat the baby orangutan, Buffy.

When I got to the zoo and examined him, it was clear that the little guy had severe gastroenteritis and was dehydrated. I immediately put him on some special baby stuff we used for infants his age when they were this dehydrated and hoped I wouldn't have to start an IV on him. Of course, I had to see him every day for weeks, to ensure he was improving and little Buffy grew to love me because I also made him feel better. He improved quickly and, when I would come, he would jump into my arms and cuddle. I was so happy for those few weeks.

When the zoo staff saw how I handled Buffy, they asked me if I would see the gorilla too.

Would I? Absolutely. And so I met Caroline, the sweet gorilla, and her not-so-sweet, feces-throwing male counterpart, Tuffy. Caroline would allow me to examine her belly and her head. I would tickle her nose through the bars. I invented a special audio stethoscope for the staff to use—they wanted to be able to tell if Caroline was pregnant and wanted to listen for a fetal heart rate. My new stethoscope worked very well. You might ask why I didn't use ultra sound or other instruments like that. The answer is simply that they were not invented yet, and if they were, were certainly not in common usage. So my little audible stethoscope was all they had, but it did work, so they were pleased.

I managed to stay connected to the zoo staff for several months but I was working hard at the hospital and I didn't have the time to keep running out to the zoo, as much as I loved going there. I suppose I could have been a vet but, truthfully, I love talking to patients. I would sometimes sit for a long time and just let a patient talk and talk—fascinated by everything she or he would say. I don't speak ape or dog well enough to be a vet. But English, that I could manage.

1974-1975
Second Year of Residency

AFTER DR. SATLAND had vetoed my request to work on the hospital ship, I had to find something to do for an elective for three months. Dr. Fisher, a dermatologist and excellent physician, had asked me if I would come work with him in Israel for three months. He alternated doing medicine in Calgary and Israel and thought three months there would be an interesting experience for me. I asked him if Joanne could also do an elective there, and before I could blink, Joey and I were landing in Israel beginning a three month elective at Tel Hashomer, a hospital just outside of Tel Aviv.

I have to say it was a refreshing break from my struggles at University of Calgary. Dr. Fisher gave me a special project to work on, aside from seeing patients, of course, and left me to it. I had been to Israel six years previously, but this time I was coming not as a tourist but as a doctor, to work and to learn. The first day I arrived, I got my name tag, which said Dr. Simkin in Hebrew. I was so proud of that. People treated me like a doctor, a very different experience than Calgary.

My cousin Jackie was living in Israel at the time, in Natanya, which was fairly close to our hospital, Tel Hashomer. Joanne and I had a small room at the hospital, and a larger room at cousin Jackie's where we spent most weekends. Jackie's place was in a large high-rise right on the beach. The situation worked out very well for us. We spent four or five days a week in total chaos at the hospital, and the other two or three days relaxing at Jackie's or going on *tiuls* (tours) with Jackie's friend Ofra, who was a Sabra (Israeli born) and seemed to know everybody in and every inch of the country. Both Joanne and I, like everyone else in Israel, loved Ofra.

The hospital was hectic for sure. I remember one day walking down the hall and a man ran up to me and pulled his pants down, wanting me to look at some hidden part of his anatomy. I just kept on walking. Patients would sneak into the office and try to move their chart from the bottom of the pile to the top. There were many languages spoken, shouted actually, often all at the same time. It was noisy, chaotic, and mostly fun. I learned a lot about people and a fair bit of medicine. And we saw much of the country while we were there. Different from working on a hospital ship, for sure, but, thanks to Dr. Satland, I had an unusual and replete three months in Israel.

Joey and I were exploring the old city in Jerusalem, walking in the Arab quarter, dressed appropriately of course, with long everythings. But we were still two women alone. We found ourselves on a narrow road when we came across a group of Arab youths.

"Hey, *Americanas*," they yelled, sneering. One picked up a stone and lobbed it towards us. We ignored them. But when a second stone came perilously close, we turned around. They were all laughing and picking up stones, getting ready to throw them at us. At the first stone that came a little too close for comfort, Joanne leaned over, picked up her own stone and, in championship first-base softball form, hurled it at the ringleader where it hit him hard on the leg. He yelped loudly, hopping on one foot, holding his leg. The boys dropped their stones and ran. Joanne and I quickly exited the Arab quarter.

Only one other incident marred the otherwise wonderful time in Israel. We were in a small Arab town near the Syrian border, working at a clinic there. During my lunch break, I decided to wander around the town. In those days, I loved making little movies. Now, Sophie, this was way before cell phones and portable cameras. I had a huge video camera that I lugged around on my shoulder and actually made some fine travel films, which I had to edit by cutting the film and splicing by hand.

I came across two elderly gentlemen playing backgammon, or *shesh besh* as they called it, on a small table outdoors on the street. They were Arabs, wearing the common headdresses called *keffiyeh*—cotton scarves wound around their heads. They were both concentrating very hard and I thought they both looked wonderfully interesting, so I began to film them from across the street. One of them looked up and saw me. He yelped as he leaped up, knocking his chair over backwards and, before I knew it, both of them were chasing me down the street. I ran as fast as I could, lugging my camera, and got to the clinic and slammed the door just seconds before they got there.

They both were shouting, pounding on the door, and waving their hands at me. It was clear that they were very unhappy.

"What are they saying?" I asked one of the nurses to translate.

"The men, they are unhappy. They say you interrupt their game. They say no woman ever take picture of men. Bad thing to do."

"Oh, I'm so sorry. I had no idea."

The nurse looked through the window in the door, listening to their angry shouts.

"They no care you sorry. They mad. They want to hurt you. Go in other room. They leave soon."

I did and they did.

We had a wonderful three months, working in Tel Aviv, Jerusalem, and a nearby Arab village, and touring around the country on extended week-ends. I did some research, learned a little dermatology, and a lot about Israel. I could breathe easier and I came back much refreshed and ready for my medical work.

When the three months were over, Dr. Fisher asked me to write a paper on the research I had done. I did and it was published under both our names. Shortly after I got back to Canada, I was asked to present it at an international conference in Banff. I guess it was a big deal.

I had been working on the treatment for basal cell epithelioma of the vulva. The treatment at that time was total excision of the vulva; in other words, doctors were cutting away women's genitals, a terribly disfiguring and distressing procedure. I discovered that wasn't necessary and treatment was better under local excision. As a result of my work, the global treatment for vulvar epithelioma changed and, instead of massive, mutilating surgery in usually unsuccessful attempts to treat it, the treatment of choice became minimal local excision and most women recovered very well without the disfiguring surgery. After I presented the paper at Banff a few months after I returned, I received an award for this discovery. I was very pleased but, of course, my medical school minimized it as much as they could.

IN TERMS OF my personal life, major changes were occurring. Upon our return from Israel, Joanne and I were both under a lot of stress from our residencies and studying, and we decided to separate. We remained friends, but she moved out of the house. I became very depressed because I wasn't sure how I felt about this. I thought it was a good thing for us to split but I missed her terribly.

My mother was visiting me one day, and as I puttered in the kitchen, she asked, "Ruthie, what's wrong? You seem unhappy, something is bothering you. What's the trouble?"

"Oh, Mom, you really don't want to know." I looked up at her.

"Well, would you rather I go on having my suspicions all these years?"

And that's when I told my mom, who obviously already knew, that I was a lesbian.

I took a deep breath. "Okay, Mom, Joanne and I broke up. I'm a lesbian."

My mom nodded slowly and said, "I just hope you can be less depressed. Is there anything that can make you happier, Doctor?" She smiled at me.

"Just tincture of time." I smiled back.

I want you to know, Sophie, that my mom was always very supportive. I do have to say that my entire family treated my partners as just that—partners. While I think they would have preferred I not be a lesbian, they were all very understanding. My family all liked Joanne and it was hard for them when we split up. But they were supportive of me and still friendly to Joanne when they saw her.

I had told my sister, your grandmother, earlier, when I first moved to Calgary. She and her first child, your aunt Roberta, came to visit me. Your mother wasn't yet born. I picked them up at the airport. Roberta was still an infant in arms. As we were driving home, I had decided to tell my sister about my being a lesbian. It used to be a big thing. We were driving home in my little orange Fiat convertible. My hands were tightly gripping the steering wheel and I took a deep breath.

"Uh, Judi, er, I, um, I have, er, something to tell you."

"What?" She sat up, a look of concern upon her face.

"Um, I think I'm a homosexual."

She smiled. "Oh shit, Ruth, I've known that for years."

And that was that.

I don't know what the next big silent thing in the world will be, Sophie, but if you ever have something that you feel you need to hide, I encourage

you to rethink that. It is never a good idea to live with a lie. Tell the truth and
deal with the consequences. You will feel a lot lighter and you will be surprised
by the support you receive. Some things feel so big. It feels to us as though it
would be impossible to tell our family or our friends some of our secrets. But,
Sophie, take a deep breath and start talking. In the end, you won't regret it.
It's true, I kept the fact that I was a lesbian mostly under wraps while I was in
medical school. I didn't come out fully until I was in my own medical office.
But that was because I was trying to minimize the number of things for which
Dr. Satland *et al* could hassle me. I felt that, if I were an out lesbian in school,
it would just be one more reason for them to try to kick me out. The first day
in my own medical office, all of that left me. I didn't think they could get me.
Of course, I was a bit too optimistic about that but, still, no regrets.

OVERALL I ENJOYED my residency tremendously. Even Dr. Saunders
seemed to develop a certain respect for me. I was beginning to feel part of a
team caring for patients, and not so much as an outsider.

One day, Irene, one of the head nurses at the Family Practice Clinic walked
up to me.

"Ruth, we are starting this new program and we wondered if you would
help us with it. We're calling it Trym Gym. It's a weight loss program and it is
going to last four months. We would like you to do one of the first lectures on
medical problems of obesity, and then another session towards the end of the
program. Can you help us with this?"

I have always had a problem with my weight, something I inherited
honestly from my dad. I was either gaining weight or losing weight but was
rarely at the same weight for any length of time. When Irene approached me,
I was on the high end of the weight scale.

"Irene, why are you asking me? I'm fat. Why not ask one of the skinny
residents?"

"We want you, Ruth. We think you will be very good."

"Well, Irene, the only way I could do that is if I actually go on the program
too. It's not right to have a fat doctor talking about medical problems of
obesity. Who would believe me?"

"So you'll do it then?" Irene asked. "You'll do the program with us?"

"Well, I'll do the lectures and I'll lose the weight, but I'm not coming every week. But I'll lose the weight to show them I'm serious and that it can be done."

And so I gave a lecture to thirty-three fat women, who were sitting in the room looking at me and wondering why a fat doctor was talking to them.

"I know what you must be thinking." I perched against the table. "Why would I be believable? Well, I'll tell you this. Being fat is really not terribly cool and it's not healthy. So to prove how serious I am, I will lose weight with you. This program goes on for several months, but I won't see you again until the last few weeks of the program. And in four months, we will all be successful with our weight loss, okay?"

A few of the women nodded. They weren't too sure. But I knew that in order to be a credible physician, I really had to lose a lot of weight over the next few months. And I worked hard at that while I also worked hard in the clinic, seeing my family practice patients.

In the meantime, I continued to see patients and I worked longer hours than most.

"Hello, Mr. Thompson, how are you today?" I walked into the room to see an elderly gentleman, eighty-three years old, seated in the chair with both hands leaning on the top of his brown, wooden cane.

"Mr. Thompson?" He looked at me quizzically.

"Mr. Thompson, hello." I gently touched him on the shoulder. He just looked at me. I stood right in front of him, leaned in front of his face, and asked a bit louder, "Mr. Thompson, do you hear okay?"

"Eh, what's that?"

"Hear!" I shouted. "Can you hear okay?"

"Oh yes, no problem. Why do you ask?"

"Well, what's been troubling you?"

"Eh? What's that?"

"Troubling you." I cranked the volume up yet again. "What's the problem?"

"Oh. I've been throwing up."

"Throwing up, you say?"

"I'm hungry but my stomach don't want the food."

"Oh, for how long have you been throwing up?"

"What's that?"

"How long?" I shouted.

"For two weeks."

"When did it start?"

"At home." It wasn't always the easiest thing to elicit relevant information. After I dealt with Mr. Thompson, I saw Mr. Elgin.

"Hello," I said, as I walked into the room. A gentleman in a brown cardigan sweater, shirt and tie stood up.

"I had only one eye and my other eye wasn't very good. You betcha. And then doctor, ya' know, it hurts when I put my finger in my ear. Yup. And I have sit-itis, you betcha. Yup."

"Hmm, okay," I said. After I was finished with Mr. Elgin, I went into another examining room to do a physical on a twenty-three-year-old woman.

"When was your last menstrual period?" I asked.

"Four months ago," was the reply.

"Could you be pregnant?"

"I don't know."

"What do you mean, you don't know?"

"My regular doctor is on vacation."

I loved virtually every one of my patients. They opened up the world for me. I continued with the physical. She was lying on the examination table and I was palpating her abdomen.

"What operation is that?" I asked, running my finger along a scar on her right side.

"My God bladder."

"Hmm. When did that come out?"

"Let's see," she thought, "after this one" and she pointed to another scar on her lower abdomen.

"And what operation was that?"

"A Zarian," was the reply.

I often felt I spoke several languages when I saw patients; English, and Patient Medicalese, which was its own lingo, containing such expressions as Arthur-it-is, appendage attack, and one of my personal favourites, a high anus hernia.

"Ruth," Marlene stopped me as I came out of an examining room, "there is an extra patient here today, Mrs. Kovacs. She's a sixty-seven-year-old woman who wants to see a doctor to have her blood pressure checked. Will you see her?"

"Sure, Marlene, put her in a room and I'll be right there."

A few minutes later, I walked into the examining room, where Mrs. Kovacs was sitting in a chair, brown purse on her lap, black hat with a little floral arrangement on it perched on her head, grey dress, with a maroon scarf around her neck.

"Hello, Mrs. Kovacs." I smiled at her. "What can I do for you today?"

"I would like you to check blood pressure."

"Okay, no problem. Do you not have your own doctor?"

"Oh yes, I do. I have a good doctor, but I didn't want to bother him. You check pressure for me?"

I smiled at her. "Of course I can," I said, but I thought something else. Why was it okay for her to "bother" me but not her own doctor?

I approached to put the blood pressure cuff on her arm and was almost physically repelled backward by the strong halitosis coming from her. I found that I was holding my breath so I did not have to inhale.

"You know, Mrs. Kovacs, maybe you should see your own doctor. You are more than welcome to come here, but it's important you see the same doctor if possible. That way, we can help you better."

Mrs. Kovacs nodded.

"You can decide if you would like to come here or go to your own doctor," I continued, "but I think you should pick one place and go there for all the visits. Okay?"

Mrs. Kovacs nodded.

"You weigh me?" she asked.

"Sure," I said, indicating with my arm the scale against the wall. "Just come stand over here." I weighed her.

"That's 185 pounds."

"Ach, I've got all these rags on today. Better put down 175."

Mrs. Kovacs was a strange one. She did come back to our clinic, but I don't know if she also continued seeing her "real" doctor.

Four months went by, seeing patients every day, going to rounds at the hospital, and being a doctor in the family practice clinic. I absolutely loved it! I couldn't think of anything I would rather be doing. It was almost the end of the four months, and I was due to return for my final Trym Gym talk. To keep my promise, I had worked very hard on my own weight loss program.

On the day of my lecture, I carried a large bag into my shared office.

"What have you got there?" Marlene asked.

"Here, give me a hand." I pulled out four shirts and four pairs of pants, all different sizes, and with Marlene's help, put them all on. I looked pretty much the same or heavier than when I first met with them four months earlier.

I walked into the room where the women were all sitting.

"Hi Trym Gym group. Don't you all look good. How do you think I look?" I turned around slowly, as if to show off my curves, which really weren't there.

There was some mumbling in the group and the women looked disappointed.

"Now, I told you I would lose weight with you. I meant it." I then removed one shirt and one pair of pants.

There were some relieved titters in the room.

"Now, do I look better?"

A few of the women nodded. I started the lecture but, after a minute or so, stopped and said, "I can see that some of you don't think I've kept up my part of the bargain. I don't want to disappoint you. I think I'll take this off." I removed another blouse and another pair of pants. There was a bit more laughter in the room, and I continued with the lecture. After another five minutes: "It's warm in here, isn't it? Better take this off." I removed the third blouse and pair of pants. Now the women were more relaxed and relieved. "You know, I wouldn't let you down. If I said I was going to do this with you, I meant it." I then removed the last layer of clothing, showing them that I had indeed lost forty-seven pounds during that time.

Over the years, my weight continues to be unstable but I have completely had a change of heart about obesity. Although it is much easier physically for me when I weigh less, I can't always weigh what I would like to, so I have learned to accept how I am. My goodness as a person is not dependent upon the number on the scale, as I once thought. It is what it is.

I learned another lesson which I wish to impart to you, Sophie: Don't waste valuable time in your life trying to make yourself into something you are not. For some people, trying to lose weight or gain weight is akin to trying to grow six inches taller. It ain't gonna happen. Do what you can reasonably do and accept the rest.

I WAS NOW in my last few months of my family practice residency. We were approaching the end of the school year, and I would need to sit my CCFP exams for my Family Practice Specialty Certification. We were supposed to register to sit this exam between certain dates. Those dates coincided with when I would be overseas in Israel, so before I left, I asked Dr. Cox, who dealt with the residents, what I should do.

"Oh, don't worry, Ruth. You go off to Israel for your elective. I'll register you with the others when the time comes. There is nothing to worry about." He was very reassuring, and I took him at his word. I went off to Israel, confident that all was in order.

Two months after I returned from Israel, the other residents were all talking about letters they had received telling them where to go for the exams. Letters? What letters? I quickly realized I was the only resident who had not received one of these letters.

"Dr. Cox." I urgently knocked on his door.

"Oh, hi, Ruth. What can I do for you?" He indicated a chair beside his desk and I sat down.

"Remember before I went to Israel, you said you would register me for the CCFP exams. I didn't get any notification from them. Did you not register me?"

"Oh no, Ruth, did we forget to tell you?" He looked distraught. "We thought about the times you had been away ill. Since this was the first year University of Calgary students will be taking these exams, we didn't want any chance of having our averages brought down, so decided not to register you. Perhaps you can try for next year." He smiled sadly at me.

"What are you talking about? I'm an A student. I've always had good marks."

"Yes, perhaps." He smiled again. "But you were ill for a while, and we didn't want that to negatively impact our overall school grade."

"Negatively impact? Are you crazy? Okay, never mind, I'll just register now," I said and got up to leave the office.

"I'm afraid that's impossible, Ruth. The deadline for registration was three weeks ago."

"Maybe you can tell them you made an error, and they will let me register."

"That's not possible. We have decided you should not write these exams."

"But you have no basis for making this decision."

He smiled again, and I just wanted to slap his smiley face until it stopped that idiotic grinning.

"Sorry. There's nothing you can do."

I stormed out, furious. Did these guys *never* give up? But I would not admit defeat, not at this late date. I called some professors who had been supportive of me in the past, but every one told me that since the registration date had passed, there was nothing anyone could do.

Then I spoke with lawyers, other doctors, and was on my way to Ottawa to talk with the committee there, when Dr. Blackburn, from the General Hospital, called me back.

He had always been one of my supporters and was furious when he found out what had happened. He was actually on the committee for the CCFP exams, and was leaving the next day for Ottawa.

"Just leave it with me, Ruth. Give me a few days. I'll see what I can do. It wasn't right, what they did."

"Thank you, Dr. Blackburn. Please sir, please, I have to sit those exams."

"Yes, I know you do. Just give me a few days. I'll get back to you."

And sure enough, three days later, Dr. Blackburn called from Ottawa.

"Ruth, it was not easy, but we managed to get you into the CCFP boards with the rest of your class. You'll be taking the exams with the others."

This was one of the very few times in the past five years my tears flowed from relief and happiness. If Dr. Blackburn hadn't been in Ottawa, I would have kissed him.

The exams were three days long. They were a combination of written, oral, and role playing with patients. I have always liked exams and I enjoyed these. For me, the best part was when the results came. Dr. Cox told me that he and the other doctors did not want my marks bringing down the school average. I was in the 98th percentile in Canada. In Canada! So much for my disgracing my medical *alma mater*.

HAVING OFFICIALLY PASSED my family practice specialty exams, I couldn't wait to get out of there and to open my own practice. We finished at the end of June, 1975, and by July 1, I was ready to move into my own office. I found a place that was perfect. The Westbrook Centre had several doctors' offices, a lab, an x-ray office, and was half-way between my home and the hospital. It was ideal.

I called the Department of Family Practice to see what I had to do to get hospital privileges, so that I could start practicing medicine. I had to leave a message with the secretary. Dr. Saunders returned my call.

"Hello, Ruth. This is Dr. Saunders. As you know, I'm the head of Family Practice at Foothills Hospital. I understand that you have applied for hospital privileges with our department."

"Yes, sir, that's correct, when can I start?"

"Wait a minute. I'm afraid it's not that easy. You can't just get privileges. You need to be in a practice with doctors who already have privileges here."

Would it never end?

"What? When did that happen? That's a new rule—what's going on? I just want to practice medicine. Why are you guys doing this?"

"We're not doing anything. You are correct, it may be a new rule, but the rule still stands. In order to get privileges, you would have to be in a practice with doctors who already have their privileges."

"No, I want to work on my own. I don't want to go in with other doctors."

"That's fine, Ruth, but then you will have to practice without hospital privileges."

In 1975, that was not a viable option. I had trained to be a family physician, passed all my exams, met all my requirements, and now this rule magically surfaced just as I requested privileges preventing me from going into my own practice. That day, as I lay across my bed sobbing, I cried longer and harder than at any other time. The thought of going in with male doctors was something I could not wrap my head around.

After I was all cried out, I thought about my options, which seemed pretty limited. If no one else was ever going to cheer for me, I might as well become my own cheering section. "Okay, Ruth," I told myself, "you can do it. You can." I thought I could go in with some guys, start my own practice, or not. Simple, really.

So there's another lesson, Sophie: When you feel as though you are trapped and there is nowhere to go, there is usually a very simple solution right in front of you. Yoda really knew what he was talking about when he said, "Do. Or do not. There is no try."

So off I went to talk with Barry and Gregg, two doctors who were just down the hall from the offices where I wanted to work. Barry had been in practice about five years, and Gregg two years. We knew each other from the hospital and I explained that I wanted to start working right away. I understood almost immediately that they were interested in the rent I would be paying them to work out of their offices. So we all benefited. And, I was extremely pleased to be the very first person from the University of Calgary Medical School to go into private practice. I so do love firsts!

1975
First Year of Medical Practice

THE FIRST DAY I went to the hospital not as a student, not as a resident, but as an actual staff physician, I went into the Doctors' Lounge, which finally had a tiny washroom for women built out of a section of the existing coat rack area. The coat rack had many white coats available but I didn't like wearing white coats nor did I need to walk around with a stethoscope around my neck to advertise who I was. However, it might not have been such a bad idea.

When I walked into a four-bed room to see a patient, I heard, "Nurse, nurse," a man in one of the other beds cried out. "Quick nurse, I need a bedpan."

"Nurse!" the old man yelled at me. "Nurse, come here!"

"Sir, I am a doctor, not a nurse, but I will gladly find your nurse for you."

"Nurse, please." He sighed. "Just bring me a bedpan."

So I did.

Almost every day, I was mistaken for a nurse or some other staff person. But that was okay with me. If I didn't look like a doctor, it was because I was doing something new and different and I thought that was a good thing. So I brought bedpans, picked things up, and did other things that nurses do all the time because, to me, it was worth it not having to wear a white coat like other doctors. I didn't care if they thought I was a nurse. Well, I actually did care—it seemed impossible for people to recognize that young women could be physicians. I felt the white coats were a uniform that did not appeal to me and I took them off whenever I could. Most of my colleagues liked being recognized as DOCTOR. I just wanted to *be* a good one.

As I was getting ready to go into private practice so was Betty Flagler. And, like Tess Trueman before her, she had stellar qualifications. Not only did she complete her Ob/Gyn residency in fine form, she also had two extra years in Gynecological Oncology from Toronto. Still, the gynecologists at the hospital didn't want her to have privileges. Apparently, they were afraid of the competition. Betty was an excellent physician and surgeon, serious about her work, so caring and gentle with her patients, and there were a lot of people waiting to come see her. The male gynecologists said she didn't have much experience, which was decidedly untrue. I wrote letters of support for her but, coming from me, I don't suppose they were very helpful. I wasn't exactly the star doctor around there. After much aggravation, Betty finally got full privileges and had a very successful practice. But no new male gynecologist had to go through what Betty did, that's for sure.

I loved when we were both in private practice. We referred a lot of patients to each other. Every Wednesday morning, she would operate at the Grace Hospital, a women's hospital in the city, and I would be her surgical assistant. I loved those Wednesday mornings. We were all women: the anaesthetist, the nurses, Betty the surgeon, me the surgical assist, and, of course, the patient. We would have light classical music playing softly enough so we could all talk comfortably while we worked. It was a calm, pleasant, mostly fun, fully female atmosphere.

Sometimes I would look around and feel thrilled and proud that we were all women doing extremely specialized and difficult work, and doing it very well indeed.

DURING MY LAST year in medical school, as one of the very few female physicians, I was inundated with requests to participate in women's events and speak on panels and at conferences. My answer was always the same: right now I had to concentrate on getting through medical school and my residency but, once I was finished with my studies, I would be happy to participate.

Now having finished my residency, I was finally free to participate in the community and join some organizations. I was delighted to become an active board member, not just a chair filler, of the Board of Directors of the Calgary Birth Control Association. It was my first Board as a physician and I felt proud to be there.

Being in medical school and residency did not prevent me from automatically correcting people who only used masculine terms when they meant both men and women. I was often asked what the big deal was, and why did I keep saying that I was a feminist?

Well, Sophie, it was a big deal, and unfortunately, it still is. I say unfortunately, because I would have hoped that issues would be more resolved now than they are. But when little girls and young ladies and women always hear words in the masculine, it becomes difficult to see men and women as equal. "Of course the word men means both men and women," people would say—I was sick of hearing that. If it meant men and women, then say so.

I was often the only female physician at rounds at the hospital where the speaker would start by saying, "Gentlemen", or "Gentlemen . . . and Ruth" followed by a chuckle, and always hearing doctors referred to as "he."

At a big Status of Women Conference in the late 1970s, someone had asked a government minister a rather intelligent question and he responded by saying, "My dear . . ."

"Don't call me 'dear'!" the questioner shot out.

"But, honey, I don't mean anything by it."

Can you imagine something like that happening if it were all men? Most guys just never got it. But it wasn't only the men. Many women were known to say, "I'm not a feminist, but . . ." Why on earth were they *not* a feminist? All that meant was that they believed in equal rights for men and women, socially, economically, in every way, just equal rights. Not more and not less, either. And women still insist on using the phrase, "as a rule of thumb," not knowing or caring where it came from. It comes from Old English Law, where it was stated that it was legal for a man to beat his wife as long as the stick was no thicker than his thumb. More recently, in 2017, Russia decriminalized domestic violence, so men can beat their wives with impunity. The woman has no protection. Adrienne Rich, an American poet and feminist has said, "No woman is really an insider in the institutions fathered by masculine consciousness." Since society is founded on patriarchy, is it no wonder then that every institution in it is patriarchal and rejects the equality of women? It was recently discovered that since 2011, a Japanese Medical University manipulated entrance exam results only for women in order to keep the female medical student population down. This started only after female applicants had of course distinguished themselves. There are times I just get so livid, so angry, that people cannot see how unfair all this is to women who have been brought up to be subservient to men.

You may ask why we can't just work on one issue at a time, like trying to get equal pay for work of equal value, or stopping men from physically abusing women, or any of the many other issues involved in feminism. Every single individual issue is related to feminism as a whole. Only when we have equal pay for work of equal value will women be in a position to make other financial decisions regarding child care and houses for battered women, and so forth. Women can't leave abusive husbands if welfare isn't standardized and they are unable to live. We need good medical policies so that women don't end up living their lives as caretakers. All these issues come together under the mantle of feminism—equality politically, socially, economically, culturally—equality between women and men in every way. It all fits together.

I was and am proud to be a feminist. Being a feminist was the only thing that made sense to me, even when some conservative magazines in Alberta printed some very offensive and mocking words and cartoons about me in the 1970s and 80s. I didn't care. What could be wrong with doing what you felt was right? How could it not be right to believe that everyone, women and men, were equal? Really, that's all feminism is—equality in every aspect of our lives, social, political, economic. I could never understand why people say the word "feminist" like it is a disgusting word.

Sophie, one thing I truly would like you to remember is that I was a strong feminist all of my life. I would be more than proud if you became a feminist as well. I would like that word "feminism" to be obsolete now, but I don't think it will be in my lifetime. I hope that you and other young women will agree that women and men should be equal in all areas of life and work hard to help make that happen. It sounds like such an obvious thing—equality. Why ever not? But in this, the first half of the twenty-first century, true equality between women and men does not exist.

I truly hope, Sophie, that you and your friends incorporate equality into your lives, and that it becomes a non-issue, not something that needs to be fought for over and over again. But every time I hear "men" for both women and men, or "you girls," or some strange man calls me "dear" or "honey," I cringe. Still. Although it's an uncomfortable feeling, I hope that you feel the same way, and don't let people get away with sloppy pronouns and muddled means of addressing you. Even if language seems like a small issue, fight for equality in language as much as in work, law, medicine, all of life. Women are indeed equal to men. Some might say more than equal, but we won't get into that issue right now.

AFTER I JOINED the Board of Directors of the Calgary Birth Control Association, I was asked to participate on a panel about abortion held at the Old Y, which was a community building housing many of the activist groups in the city. The moderator was a pleasant enough guy named Bill, and there were four of us on the panel. One of the panelists was an elegant, blonde psychologist named Maria. I knew none of the other speakers and very few of the audience members. Nevertheless, I offered some strong viewpoints on women's rights to choose what they needed for their own bodies. Maria and I seemed to hit it off and after the panel, we sat off in a corner talking. It turned out the moderator Bill was Maria's husband and he joined us after a while. Maria told me about the Calgary Status of Women Action Committee (SWAC) of which she was chairperson. I explained that I had been asked to participate earlier but had to finish medical school first. Maria invited me again and, within weeks, I found myself on the Board of Calgary's SWAC. Not long after, I joined the Board of Directors of the Alberta Status of Women Action Committee.

Most of the meetings for Calgary SWAC were at Maria and Bill's home, although Bill usually made himself scarce for the meetings. After the first few meetings, I was curious about something. Although everyone said they needed more money for programs, for offices, for staff, and much more, the main suggestion they could come up with for fund raising was bake sales. After listening to this discussion for several weeks, I exploded during one meeting.

"Why are you talking about bake sales? What's wrong with you women? We need money. Lots and lots of money! You can't raise that selling muffins. Look, I just read about the provincial lotteries for casinos. Groups like ours can apply to the government, and if we are accepted, we can hold a casino where we could earn tens of thousands of dollars."

"We can't do that," Joan interjected.

"Why not?"

"Because we have to be responsible for the whole thing."

"So?" I asked.

"Are you prepared to be responsible for running an entire casino?"

"Sure. Aren't you? How else are you going to get enough money?"

We argued about this for weeks. I brought all the forms to the meeting. Most of the women were terrified to sign their names to something holding them responsible not only for running the casino but also for the finances.

"Look. We have to try. Why not give it a go? All we've got to lose is all our money."

A groan filled the room. "I think Ruth is right," Maria said softly. "We should at least try. Let's fill out the forms and see what happens."

One month later, at a SWAC meeting held at Maria's house, I brandished a large manila envelope.

"It's here. We got it. We won the lottery. We can have our casino."

"Great," Francis said. "Now what?"

"Now, we organize it," I said.

"Have you ever done that before?"

"No, but how hard can it be?"

A few weeks later, Maria was at my house, drinking a glass of scotch on ice.

"Don't tell the group," I confided, "but organizing this casino is a hell of a lot harder than I thought it would be."

Maria smiled.

"We'll do fine, though," I continued. "We just need to organize everyone for the two evenings of the casino. We need runners and chippies and counters and all kinds of folks. We'll have enough people from our group. It should be fun."

Maria smiled again. She seemed to smile a lot when she and I were together.

"Enough about the casino. Tell me more about yourself." I held up my rye to clink glasses with Maria. I learned about Maria's first husband Ed, and Bill, her current husband. I wanted to know more about her work, as head of Psychology at one of the city's hospitals.

"Too bad we don't work at the same hospital, Maria. Then we could have our coffee breaks together. Oh wait—I forgot. Doctors don't have time for coffee breaks. I haven't had a coffee break in years." We laughed.

"You have some of the most amazing furniture," Maria commented, brushing her hand over the brown suede sofa.

"Yeah, that's one of my favs." I smiled. "The round, brown thing. Lots has happened on this round brown thing. Lots."

"Like what?" Maria asked. She was sitting on the edge of the sofa, sensuously rubbing the soft brown suede.

"Well, like this." And I slowly and gently leaned over and kissed her. To my amazement, Maria kissed me back. More than once.

Running the casino was a lot of fun but not as much fun as watching the faces of the women when I reported that in those two days we had made over sixty thousand dollars for SWAC.

"I have to go up to Fort MacMurray to give a seminar in a few weeks," Maria told me on one of our extended visits.

"Need help?"

"Not really. But maybe you could give a health seminar while I do my status of women presentation."

"Sounds like a plan to me. Would we be gone for the week-end?"

Maria smiled and leaned back into the round brown thing, waiting for the kiss to seal the deal.

"Wow, our first trip together." I loved being on the small prop plane which was headed up north. "How exciting. Where are we staying?"

"I think there is only one motel. Anyway, we have a room there."

Once we got there, I wanted to go exploring. "It's like trailer city. Everything is a trailer. The pub is a trailer. The restaurant is a trailer. The schools are trailers, the buildings are trailers, even the trailers are trailers." I laughed. "I can hardly believe it."

"Believe it. This is Fort MacMurray." Annie came to meet us at the plane and was driving us around. After a quick dinner in the pub, we decided to go to our room to prepare our presentations for the next day. It seemed as though every room in that hotel other than ours was on heavy duty party mode. After the fifth phone call to the front desk asking if the noise could be kept down just a little (apparently it couldn't), we gave up. Neither one of us slept well, with drunken men thumping the walls all around us.

"This is not exactly the romantic week-end I had envisioned," I grumbled.

"Let's get some sleep," Maria murmured.

"Our first week-end together." I shrugged. "Life can sure be funny at times."

Both our presentations were very successful and the women wanted to take Maria and I out for dinner and to party. It seemed as though Fort MacMurray was continuously in party mode.

Upon returning to Maria's house in Calgary, we found Bill and another woman talking in the living room.

"Pat! What are you doing here?" Maria exclaimed as she hugged her.

"Ruth, this is my best friend, Pat. She and her husband Wynn used to live together with Bill and me."

"Hi." I waved. "Well, I guess I should go and let you visit."

"No, stay. Have a drink." This from Bill. I did and quickly became part of their family.

I HAD STARTED working in Barrie and Gregg's office as soon as possible, and worked Tuesdays, Thursdays, and Fridays, sharing call every third night. Not exactly what I had wanted, but it was a start.

I was busy right from the beginning. It seemed that many women in Calgary had been waiting for a female family doctor. After six weeks, I was seeing more patients than either Barry or Gregg. I asked if I could have any more time working in the office, but they understandably were reluctant to give up their patient time. I started coming into work earlier and earlier in the mornings, and by the fourth month, I knew that I would have to have an office where I could work at least five days a week. Barry and Gregg were nicer than I expected but, with our current arrangement, I just couldn't work enough hours.

Barry and Gregg figured that if I had an office near them, then they could perhaps pick up some of the overflow. We would all benefit with my moving down the hall into my own place. So Barry went to talk to Dr. Saunders. I am not sure exactly what took place and, truthfully, I didn't care. I only knew that, finally, I could get my own office and maintain my hospital privileges.

I immediately rented the office that very kindly had remained empty waiting for me during the time I was at Barry and Gregg's and designed it to be a two person medical office.

I designed my own charts, because I could not find any that represented how I wanted to run my practice. For example, all patients who came for physicals were asked if they had ever been depressed, or physically or sexually abused, questions they likely had never been asked before.

The waiting room displayed magazines such as Ms. and Herizons as well as the Calgary Women's Newspaper and the book *Our Bodies, Ourselves*. There was a large cork board with notices for current lectures, workshops, concerts, and anything else relevant to women that was going on in the city, plus business cards of female lawyers, realtors, accountants, most of whom were patients. The colours of the walls, carpets, and furniture were warm and welcoming. Even the art work was different. A friend and patient was an art instructor at the Alberta College of Art and her students painted a large mural on the wall.

I could dress the way I wanted to in my own office which usually meant jeans, T-shirts, and socks with no shoes. Very different than my grandmothers, your great-great-grandmothers, whose offices were kitchens and whose uniforms were aprons. Medicine can be a rigid discipline, and I hated to be controlled. I especially didn't like organizations where I was not treated as an equal. If I wasn't going to be equal, then I chose to be unique. I stayed true to myself.

Marlene became my nurse. Maria moved into the other office and into my home after a consensual separation from Bill. After quitting her job at the General Hospital and starting a PhD program, she saw patients when she didn't have to be at the university.

"A psychologist and a family physician. What a team. Let's call it the Body and Soul Shop." And so we did.

Maria seemed to have very little difficulty deciding to leave Bill and move in with me. The interesting thing was that she did not identify as a lesbian. She said that she loved me and wanted to spend her life with me. I had considered myself as a lesbian for many years now, and my lesbian "herstory" was important to me. It had no effect on Maria and she wasn't interested in anything lesbian in the least. But she loved me and wanted to live with me.

When she first moved into my home, I was musing about how we would have parties.

"What do you mean?" she asked.

"Well, you know I go to gay and lesbian parties all the time. Your parties are with straight heterosexual couples. We'll have to have different kinds of parties and that will be awkward."

"What are you talking about?"

"Well, you can't mix straight and lesbian and gay people at a party."

"Why not?" she asked.

"Well, because, well, you just don't. We never mix—the straight people would get upset to see two men dancing or two women. I don't know, it's just not done . . ."

"Oh, Ruth, don't be silly." Maria smiled. "Here's what we'll do—we will have one big party. You invite all your friends, and I will invite all my friends. And after the party, if anyone doesn't like our household, they just won't come anymore."

And that's exactly what we did. We had a big party, over one hundred people. And it was a great party! There was only one minor incident. Jack, the ex-husband of a friend of ours, was known for always coming on to women and his hands were a little too friendly when he met good looking women. We thought of him as a sleezebag and apparently so did his wife which is why she had decided to leave him.

Charles, an extraordinarily handsome man, six feet four, thick blond hair, dressed in an elegant suit, dimples showing when he smiled which was often, stood against the wall, surveying the room. Charles had a very prestigious job at the Glenbow Museum; he was intelligent, kind, fun, and a gay man. And he politely propositioned Jack. Jack was appalled and came running into the kitchen to complain to me. I burst out laughing.

"Why are you laughing? That man was rude to me—kick him out. Get him out of here," Jack whined.

"Jack, did he touch you inappropriately?"

"Well, no, but . . ."

"So all he did was say something to you that you didn't want to hear. It's what you do to women all the time. If anyone is leaving this party early tonight, it will be you, not Charles."

Jack sputtered, stomped his feet like the immature person he was, and left. The rest of us laughed about that incident for decades.

The party was a huge success. And I learned a very valuable lesson. I was really the prejudiced one here. I had put everyone into categories and boxes, where they didn't belong. Categories don't really mean anything. Gay, straight, lesbian, blonde, fat, tall, who cares. A person is a person is a person. From that day forth, we never again isolated our gatherings with only gays and lesbians or only straight people. We invited over the people we thought we would enjoy having over. We threw all categories into the garbage where they belong. And our home hosted some pretty terrific parties.

JUST AFTER I moved into my very own office, Germaine Greer, a feminist icon from Australia, came to Calgary to speak at the University. I was already very actively involved in the feminist movement in Calgary and was looking forward to hearing her speak. I'd read her book, *The Female Eunuch*, and was enthusiastic about going to see one of my genuine heroes. I had also enrolled in Women's Studies classes at the University of Calgary. I had been in University for so long now, I couldn't conceive of not studying something. I really did like learning,

I loved Women's Studies; this was in the very early days when Women's Studies was a brand new entity. Even a year or so earlier such a thing did not exist. Unfortunately, Sophie, by the time you get to University, Women's Studies will be supplanted by Gender Studies and will likely disappear completely. Who knows what it will be called in the future, if anything at all.

In the 1970s, Women's Studies was a new field, and universities all over North America were just starting to add courses in that area. It would still be another decade and a half until a person could get a PhD in Women's Studies, so those of us who took even one course were considered to be well established in the field.

The auditorium where Greer was to speak was filled to overflowing and there were people in the hallways, sitting on the stairs, in adjacent rooms, occupying every bit of available space. The lecture was late starting because they had to set up speakers elsewhere in the building so everyone could at least hear her. I managed to squeeze into the main auditorium toward the back and was standing on my tiptoes with anticipation. There was a buzz in the room. It looked as though most people were excited as well, and everyone was smiling and seemed as pumped as I was.

Finally, Germaine Greer came to the podium. I thought she was wonderful, probably because I agreed with everything she said, and she truly was an excellent speaker. Until question period. Responding to a question, she told the many hundreds of people there to stay away from doctors because they couldn't be trusted. She continued to say many more negative things about doctors. My hero was trashing not only medicine, but me! I had not been a doctor for a full year yet, and she was telling everyone around me never to go to me, to ignore me, that I would hurt them. I worked my way up to the front, struggling to get past the hordes of people, pushing my way up to the microphone. I was furious. When it was my turn to speak, I looked straight at her and started talking.

"You are wrong!" I heard a collective gasp in the crowd. "I agree that some doctors may not be great, but some of us are trying to change things. Some of us became doctors so that we could help women. We are feminist physicians who believe we can make things better and easier for women, not harder. And you are telling everyone here to ignore us. That's not right. I work hard as a doctor and I want to make things better for women. I'm sorry your experiences have been so negative, but not all of us are bad. Some of us are trying to make a significant difference, using strong feminist principles in our practices."

When I was finished speaking, there was applause. Germaine Greer looked thoughtful, or maybe that was just my hope. I pushed my way back to where I had been standing, with people patting my shoulder and wanting to shake my hand.

After the lecture was over, I was anxious to get back to my car and go home, as I had to be at work before seven a.m. I could not get out of the parking lot.

"Wait." A young woman with a blonde ponytail grabbed my arm. "Wait. Do you have a card? Can I come see you?"

"Yeah. Do you have a card? I want to come too," another woman in a blue jacket said.

I was surrounded with people wanting to come see me.

"Look, I'm sorry," I addressed the crowd who was now all around me, "I really don't have any cards. I'm pretty new in practice. My name is Dr. Ruth

Simkin, and my office is in Westbrook Mall. I'm happy to see any of you. Just call or drop by and make an appointment. Thanks for your support." I squeezed into my orange Fiat and roared off, smiling.

Within the next few weeks, my practice was completely full. I was working five long days a week, occasionally coming in on week-ends to catch up on paperwork. And I had Germaine Greer to thank for that.

1976-1977
Second and Third Year of Medical Practice

PART OF HAVING hospital privileges involved having to participate in one of the many hospital committees, most of which held no interest for me. I would rather be seeing patients. I was still trying to "fit in" and acknowledged that being on a hospital committee was part of having hospital privileges.

I decided to offer to be on the abortions committee, so at least I would be one less man with whom the women would have to contend. In the 1970s, women who wanted abortions had to apply and then appear in front of an abortions committee. I thought it was quite barbaric having these upset, terrified women appear in front of three strange men who had power over them in life-altering ways. The one thing that held me back from applying was the chairperson of the abortions committee: Dr. Keith Pearce.

Dr. Pearce was the head of psychiatry, and a very powerful person in the hospital. He taught us in medical school and was very involved with the medical students. In fact, he was involved with everything he could get his hands on. I noticed that people kowtowed to him all the time. I tended to keep my distance, since I knew I couldn't be subservient the way I had seen others act around him.

The more I saw him, the more he repulsed me. I had an incredibly negative visceral response every time I was near him. I didn't trust him and I didn't like him. And, he was the Chair of the Abortions Committee. However, after giving the matter a great deal of thought, I decided that helping women won out over the unpleasantness of being around Dr. Pearce. So, I choose the Abortions Committee as the committee on which I would like to serve. There weren't very many other competitors for a spot on the Abortions Committee for several reasons—abortion was a very contentious topic and most people wanted to avoid any discussion about it. Also, there was the Chairperson: most people wanted to be as far away from Dr. Pearce as from the topic of abortion.

I had no trouble finding myself a member of the Abortions Committee of Foothills Hospital.

We met over noon hour once a week to go over our cases and sign them off, and the interviews with the women were then scheduled for other times.

The first few months went smoothly enough until, during one meeting, I casually remarked to the room, "CBC Radio has asked me to be on a radio show to talk about abortion."

"Asked *you*?" Pearce shouted. "Why on earth would they ask you? *I* am the chairman. I should be the one going."

"Sorry, Dr. Pearce, they asked me and I'll be there."

"We'll see about that," he mumbled.

Two days later, at 7:45 in the morning, I was walking down the hallways of CBC when Dr. Pearce came up to me.

"Why didn't you call to remind me about this?"

"Call you? Dr. Pearce, I am your colleague, not your secretary."

"Hmmph." He angrily stormed off.

"What's he doing here?" Annie, the CBC interviewer, asked me.

"Damned if I know. I didn't invite him."

"Nor did I. He called and was told we wanted you on the show. We're not crazy about having him around here."

"I can certainly understand why." I followed Annie into the interview room where Dr. Pearce was already sitting.

Annie and I had discussed on the phone what she wanted to talk about and I had some notes made. In my typical style, they were all neatly typed out, on one sheet.

Annie put the head phones on me.

"Ready?" She smiled.

"Yep. Let's do this."

After the introduction of the program, Annie said a few words and then asked, "Dr. Simkin, can we please start with your telling us how many people come for abortions every year."

"Sure, Annie." I looked down at my paper with the statistics on it, only to see it being ripped out of my hands by Dr. Pearce. Luckily, I knew the answer anyway and kept talking.

"I would like to add to that, Annie," Dr. Pearce butted in. "Dr. Simkin has not been around for very long but I, I am the chairman of the Abortions Committee."

"Yes, Dr. Pearce, I think we all know that." Annie was trying hard to be nice, but was struggling.

The whole show went like that. Annie would ask me a question and Pearce would interrupt. Between Annie and myself, we tried to make it interesting, but since we never knew what he was going to say or when, it was difficult. Plus he had all my notes, all my statistics, and would not return my sheet to me.

When the program was over, Dr. Pearce ripped off his head set and stormed out of the room, leaving my sheet sitting on the table.

"I'm sorry about that, Annie. I had no idea he was coming."

"I'm sorry too, Ruth. We have to deal with him quite often and, truthfully, I'd be happy never to see him again. You did quite well considering. Thanks. We'll be calling you again."

"Any time, Annie, my pleasure."

At one of the abortion committee meetings, I came across a familiar name. Even though I had been associated with the Calgary Birth Control Association for less than a full year, I had often come across Pat, a pro-life leader whom we met at demonstrations and lectures. She was very vocal and seemed to particularly enjoy harassing me. Pat was very actively trying to stop anything that was pro-choice. And now I saw that Pat's daughter was applying for an abortion.

I told the other committee members who she was.

"Well, maybe we should not approve the abortion," Dave said.

I shook my head. "That's just penalizing the daughter for her mother's actions. Maybe the daughter is different. One can certainly hope so."

The abortion was approved, but not before Pat came with her daughter for the interview.

After the interview, I just couldn't help myself. I just couldn't.

"Pat," I called out, as they were walking out of the hospital. "Now can you see why this is so important?"

Pat looked at me quizzically. "But this is my daughter!"

"Well, yes, but other women are other mothers' daughters too."

"That's different," Pat stated, "this is *my* daughter."

And sure enough, the week after Pat's daughter had her abortion, Pat was out trying to close us down again.

Sophie, the lesson here is don't expect people to be logical or to make sense or even to learn from a weighty situation. Often they don't, and there is just nothing we can do about that. We need to accept the way they are, whether or not that makes sense to us. And that's definitely the hardest part.

One afternoon, Maria came into my office.

"Ruth, I wonder if you could do me a favour, please?"

"Sure, Maria, what is it?"

"The husband of one of my patients is in hospital. He is very ill. He is allergic to most pain medications. The only thing that helps him is marijuana. We want you to make him some marijuana tea that he could keep in hospital."

"Oh, Maria, really, I can't do that. I just got privileges. I don't want to get into any trouble."

"Ruth, it's terrible. The man is in great pain and it's the only thing that can help him."

"Well, why involve me? Why don't you or his wife make the tea?"

"You are the only one I know who has marijuana and who knows how to make tea and how much to put in. We don't know what to do."

"Aw, Maria, I don't know. I wish you wouldn't have asked me. I want to help you out, but I just don't know . . ."

"Look, we promise to be very careful. You just make the tea and give it to me. I will give it to his wife. She will leave it at the hospital. You won't even be in the picture. Okay? Look, he really needs this. He is in so much pain."

"Okay. But please, puleeze, do not mention my name or in any other way incriminate me."

"I promise."

So I made the tea and gave it to Maria who in turn gave it to her patient, who took it to the hospital and told the nurses it was special tea for her husband that she made at home, and could they please keep it for him.

The hospital staff put the tea with his name on it in the fridge on the ward, and gave it to him when he asked for it.

A few weeks later, Maria popped her head into my office.

"You know that guy at the hospital?"

I nodded.

"Well, he is so much better. Everyone wants to know about his special tea. They can't believe how much better he is and how much his pain has improved."

I smiled.

"Thanks." She walked across the hall to her office.

AFTER MY FIRST full year of practice, I got a formal letter from the Alberta College of Physicians and Surgeons explaining that they compare different tests ordered by doctors and if any doctor uses a test much more or less than her or his colleagues (actually, they only used the masculine), they flag that test and doctor. Even though in those days it was considered standard and appropriate to do Pap tests on all women, the College told me that I did far more Pap tests during the year than my colleagues. I was asked to explain the discrepancy.

At first I was very upset. I thought of myself as a good physician, one who ordered tests appropriately. I was worried that the College had thought I was perhaps being inappropriate. Then I thought about the situation and wrote a letter back to the College, explaining that during my first year, ninety percent of my patients were women, a much higher percentage than in other practices. That was why my ordering of Pap tests was higher than my colleagues.

I didn't hear back from the College until the following year, when I got an identical letter to the one I received the previous year. By then I was getting used to things and was maybe even getting a tad jaded. I merely copied the letter I had written in the first year with a new date and sent it off. And so it went for the next few years. The College would send me the identical letter about my use of Pap tests and I would send them back my identical reply. After several years, the letters stopped coming, presumably because my practice evened out more, with more men and children coming to see me.

I WAS STILL on the Board of Directors of SWAC when we decided to sponsor a Women and Sports Conference to be held at the University of Calgary. We asked Abby Hoffman, a Canadian track and field star and Olympic athlete, to be our main speaker. Besides being well known as a star Canadian athlete, Abby was known for something else. She had learned to skate when she was very young, three years old, and by the age of nine, was eager to play hockey. There was nowhere a girl could play. She found a boys' league and registered as Ab Hoffman. Once it was discovered she was girl, she was told she was no longer welcome to play. But Abby had very cool parents, who took her case all the way to the Ontario Supreme Court. Her story was covered all over North America. After she had been playing with a boys' team for a while, she was selected as an All-Star.

I wonder, Sophie, if it seems strange to you now that a girl who is nine years old who wants to play hockey can't do it just because she is a girl. I hope that as you grow up, girls are able to do anything they want to do. But it wasn't always that way. We couldn't play the sports we wanted, couldn't wear the clothes we wanted, get the jobs we wanted, or, oh, so very many more things. Sometimes, it took going to the Supreme Court, like Abby Hoffman's family did for her to play hockey. Sometimes, different things had to happen.

Almost two hundred years ago, some women tried to stop dressing in the style of the times: a skirt dragging on the floor worn over layers and layers of starched stiff petticoats with horsehair sewn into the hems with corsets made of whale-bones that broke ribs and displaced organs. Amelia Bloomer, in her journal, *The Lily*, in 1851, printed a description for her readers on how to make the "Bloomer dress," a form of pantaloons with a shorter dress over them. This dress was considered scandalous by some. Things do change with time. I think it's important to look at things both as they are now and how they once were. Also, look at how things are now and how we want them to be in the future.

We had a great conference on Women and Sport and even had wonderful T-shirts made up. I remember my favourite was Puck Off. At the time, we thought that was very risqué. Towards the end of the conference, I wanted to do something significant that would make a change. We had heard throughout the conference about all the things that women couldn't have that men already had. For example, women's change rooms were barely adequate compared to the men's. The men even had a sauna. We decided it would be a good idea to take over the men's sauna.

It was a chilly February, but a lovely day when Abby Hoffman and some of the conference organizers walked into the sports building. We were followed by the hundreds of women who attended the conference. We walked right into the men's change room which was full of men in varying stages of undress, some even in complete stages of undress.

"What are you dames doing here? Get out!" a guy with a towel wrapped around his waist yelled at us.

"We don't have a sauna in the women's change room," I said, "so we thought we'd use yours for a while."

"Geddoudda here!" another guy yelled. "Someone get these broads outta here!"

We were all very calm and polite. We kept repeating we wanted to use their sauna. Since they had one and we didn't, we thought we could share theirs.

The TV cameras and reporters loved all of this. We made the TV news and the newspaper. There were some wonderful photos.

Being subversive can actually be a lot of fun and I loved it when we had planned "actions" like this. The women got a sauna in their change room later that year.

OFTEN WHEN WE had large conferences or award dinners or other feminist gatherings, Maria and I were very involved in arranging the specifics. Early on, it fell to me to organize the entertainment for the events. I was very happy to do that. Years went by with my organizing entertainment for large events, often more than one thousand women, before I realized I was actually producing. Once I had that realization, I started producing concerts in Calgary, almost all of them Women's Music, which was a specific genre in those days. The performers of Women's Music were almost all lesbians and were incredibly talented, albeit not so much recognized in the mainstream, with some notable exceptions. The best showcase of Women's Music, in my opinion, was the Michigan Womyn's Music Festival, which went on for forty years. I had the privilege of working there for ten summers. At our best, we had ten thousand women in the woods, and we built stages with very complex sound and lighting systems. The shows I saw there were some of the best

I have ever seen anywhere in the world and the technical knowledge was sophisticated and superior.

But in Calgary, a successful show would be a couple of hundred people. I produced shows throughout my years in Calgary, and often had posters advertising the shows in my waiting room. It was something I did in my "spare time" and I loved it. I always had a female sound engineer, most notably my good friend Nancy Poole, who also did the sound at the Day Stage at the Michigan Festival. The first time I hired Nancy, she was living in Regina and I flew her out to Calgary because I wanted an all women show. From that day on, Nancy did the sound for all the concerts I did, but it became easier because she moved to Edmonton, which was closer than Regina.

The thing is, Sophie, many times people get involved in their work and can't do or see anything else other than the work in front of them on their desks. And decades pass and they are still doing the same thing. Don't be afraid to branch out. Nancy Poole the sound engineer is also Dr. Nancy Poole, Director of BC Centre of Excellence for Women's Health and a world-recognized expert in women and addictions. Branching out. All the years I produced these concerts, I still had my medical practice. I did many different things which you will discover and managed to travel pretty much around the world as well. Personally, I am much happier when I am involved in more than one thing. I realise that is a personal choice, and it was mine. It may or may not be yours, but don't dismiss branching out unless you have a good reason. It may not appeal to you. But if it does, then do it. Try different things. Experience as much as you can. Don't put things off for later. Later may not come for you. Sadly, later does not come for many people.

I WENT INTO the examining room to see a relatively new patient, Arla, whom I had met previously at Club Carousel, but didn't know very well. I asked her how she and her partner, Ella, were doing. Arla shook her head and looked at me.

"Not too good, Doc. She was in a motorcycle accident."

"Oh no, Arla. That's terrible! Is she in hospital?"

"No, she's home now, but she's supposed to stay in bed to rest for another week or so. But you know what? I really had trouble seeing her in hospital."

"Trouble? What do you mean? What happened?"

"The police came to our home after the accident to tell me she had gone to hospital. I went down there at once and asked to see her. The nurse asked if I was a relative. I said, 'no, but we live together.' So the nurse asked again, 'But are you a relative?' I told her again, 'We live together.' She didn't understand what I meant, so she said I couldn't see her."

"Oh my goodness, Arla, what did you do?"

"I tried to stay calm. I went to sit in the waiting room and watched. When the shift changed, I waited until there was a new nurse there. Then I went up to ask if I could see Ella. She asked if I was a relative. I said, 'Yes, I am her aunt.' So she let me see her."

"What a terrible experience for you both. What can I do for you?"

"We want you to fix this. We don't want anything like this to happen to any of our friends. Can you fix it, Dr. Ruth?"

"Well, we'll give it our best shot, okay?"

I wrote a letter to the hospital board, explaining what had happened and suggesting that at this point in time, same-sex couples should not be discriminated against any more. What had happened to Ella and Arla was appalling and I would be happy to work with them to change the hospital policy regarding same-sex couples and visitation.

You see, Sophie, by this time, I was known as a lesbian crusader, sort of. I was always standing up for both women's and lesbian rights and often this was covered in the newspaper. There were times I thought my name was one long word: RuthSimkinLesbianPhysician. That longish name appeared under my photo many times in the media in the late 70s and 80s. I had also written many medical papers that were published in major medical journals like *Canadian Medical Association Journal* and *The Canadian Journal of Ob/Gyn & Women's Health Care,* papers like "Unique Health Care Concerns of Lesbians," "Not All Your Patients are Straight," "Women's Health: Time for a Redefinition," and others. I was called any time the media wanted a quote about lesbians or about something that was happening with women in the city.

Of all the things I did, there was one that I was happiest about that did not get any media coverage at all. I saw two patients in their sixties, Eileen and Mary, who had been a very closeted couple for over thirty years. They both worked in the same department at the Burns Meat Packing factory in east Calgary.

One day they came to see me together, something that was rare, because they were extremely closeted and I was one of three people who even knew that they were a couple. I had been their physician since I first went into practice.

"Good morning, Eileen, Mary. How are you two doing? What can I do for you today?" I smiled at them and rolled up on a stool to sit beside them.

Eileen was the more talkative of the two, which wasn't saying much because she usually was pretty silent.

"Uh, er, uh, we, that is . . ." She looked up at me. She was frightened and I wasn't sure why.

"What is it? It's okay. You can talk about anything here, you know that."

"Well, we've never been on a holiday together."

"What? Why not?"

"We work in the same department at work. No one there knows that we, well, you know, that we are together."

"So," Mary continued, "if one of us takes holidays, the other one has to stay at work so they won't know that we are together."

"Hmm. I see." I nodded. "That's quite a problem, isn't it?"

"Yes," Eileen said, "and you know that Mary hurt her back a few weeks ago."

Mary had come to see me for a bad back sprain. She was currently off work but was getting ready to go back in a few days.

"I am eligible for holidays now." Eileen looked sheepishly at me. "We've never been to Hawaii and we are both getting older. And Mary's back injury scared us. What if we never get a chance to go away together?"

I got it immediately. "I see. Well," I winked, "I had best check Mary's back again." I looked behind her. "Yep, just as I thought. It's necessary for you to stay off work for at least two, maybe three more weeks." I turned to Eileen. "Can you get your holiday leave immediately?"

"Yes." She nodded.

"Well, I'd better write a letter to Mary's boss and tell her Mary can't come back for three weeks. Will that be enough time for you both?"

They both nodded. "We wanted to go to Hawaii for two weeks. It will be the first time ever that we've gone away together."

I wrote out something on my prescription pad and handed it to Mary.

"I hope you both have a wonderful trip. Come see me when you return. Safe travels."

And off they went to Hawaii for two weeks, two women in their sixties, who had lived together for over thirty years, and never, ever had taken a holiday together.

You know, Sophie, I lied, something doctors really shouldn't do. It's not something any person should do. But I felt that it was important for these two women to be able to experience at least one holiday together in their lifetime and, if I could help them do that, then by golly, I would. I have absolutely no regrets.

They came to see me when they returned, all smiles and tans. They had a wonderful time. And they were thinking of changing something at work so they could have more holidays together in the future.

1978
Fourth Year of Medical Practice

AFTER TWO YEARS on the Abortions Committee, personal interviews were no longer necessary. Women requesting abortions put in an application together with their family doctor and the committee just signed off if they agreed with the request. The one thing that was necessary though was the signature of the husband.

During one meeting, Dennis, another committee member said, "I got a special request from Dr. Len Black, over at the General Hospital. It's an unusual circumstance and he is asking that we waive the husband's signature for this particular case."

"Impossible," Pearce shouted. "The husband's signature is mandatory."

"This is a special case. Both the woman and her husband are in their late thirties. Seven months ago, the husband was diagnosed with abdominal cancer and is currently at the General Hospital where he is expected to die shortly. About three months ago, the woman, in a distraught state, went out to a bar, sought comfort in the arms of a stranger, and became pregnant. She went to her family doctor, who absolutely supports her decision for an abortion but feels she should get it here instead of at the General Hospital in case her husband would accidentally find out about it. Because the husband will be dead within a month, the family physician feels the signature should be forfeited and we should support this couple in the best way we can."

"Absolutely not!" Pearce shouted. "If we don't get his signature, it will ruin our statistics."

"What?" I could stand this no longer. "Dr. Pearce, we are talking about human beings here. Human beings with a tragic story and we are in a position to help them. Are you trying to tell me that you don't care, that you won't help them because it will ruin your statistics?"

"That's exactly what I am trying to tell you," he shouted at me.

"You are even worse that I could possibly imagine. You are the most disgusting, despicable person I've ever met. I quit. I cannot work with you any longer. I absolutely refuse to be associated with this committee as long as you are on it."

"Well, good-bye to you, because everyone knows *I* am the chairman and I will be the chairman for a long time."

I got up and left the room. I just could not deal with him anymore. Yet in some ways, I really underestimated him.

I had a few psychiatric patients in my private practice who occasionally needed to be admitted, and so the nurses who worked on the psychiatric unit knew me. One of my favourite patients was Marnie, a youthful mother with a couple of young children. She was a schizophrenic who was usually pretty well controlled with drugs but every once in a while, her drugs got out of whack. At those times, we admitted her for a few days, adjusted her dose, and sent her home. We had already done that three times in the last twenty-four months, and the rest of the time she was fine.

Shortly after I quit the abortions committee, Marnie had to go back into the hospital for a few days. I admitted her on a Friday, and that week-end was one of my rare week-ends off. I wrote very specific orders for her regarding her medications and planned to discharge her on Tuesday if she was stable as I was pretty sure she would be. For some reason I can't explain, I also wrote on the order sheet: "No electric shock treatment. This patient is not to have ECT. She only needs her medications adjusted and plans are to discharge her early in the week."

Then I went off for my week-end in the mountains. When I returned early Monday morning, one of the nurses saw me getting off the elevator and ran up to me.

"Oh, Ruth, I'm so sorry to tell you this. He was here this week-end."

She didn't need to tell me who "he" was.

"What did he do?" I asked nervously.

"He shocked her," the nurse mumbled.

"What? How could he do that? I specifically wrote orders that she was not to have ECT."

The nurse held out the chart for me, which I took to the desk and started reading, trying not to let anyone see my tears.

Apparently he came in on Saturday morning, saw I had a patient, and then read the orders I wrote about not giving her shock treatments. So it only seemed like the obvious thing for him to do. The fact that this was a young woman who was well-managed on medication and didn't need shock treatments had nothing to do with it. The only reason poor Marnie got ECT was because she was my patient and I had written that order. I had failed to protect her. I discharged her from hospital as quickly as I was able and I could never apologize to her enough for what had happened. We had a strong bond; she never blamed me for this and remained my patient for many more years.

Of course, I went to see the Head of Family Practice. Of course, I issued a formal complaint against him. Of course, nothing came of it. He was Head of Psychiatry, and he told everyone that in his opinion, I was wrong and he was right and Marnie needed ECT after all. What could people do other than secretly commiserate with me and agree with him. Why he was seeing my patients in the first place when I was a staff physician in the hospital was never questioned.

About two weeks later, I was seeing another patient on the psych wards, and mumbling about Pearce to Jennie, one of the staff.

"Ya know what he did last week?" she asked me.

I raised my eyebrows in a question.

"He had been on holidays for a couple weeks, I can't remember where, but when he went into a patient's room, she said, "Oh, hi, Dr. Pearce, I haven't seen you for a couple of weeks."

"Yes, you have. I have been here every day. This just shows how sick you are and why you need to stay here."

"I almost fell over when he said that," Jennie remarked, "because I had also been there every day and he was most definitely gone."

"How does he keep getting away with all of this?" I asked.

Jenny shrugged.

I started having dreams about wanting to harm him. One day, needing to vent. I went home and wrote a letter to him. In the letter, I talked about Joan, another one of my patients. I asked him how he could be so despicable, hearing her complaint about sexual assault by an orderly and keeping her in hospital just long enough to ascertain she was not pregnant from the rape.

He then discharged and dismissed her while he and the orderly shared a sick grin. I told him they were both disgusting. And then I ranted a bit about the abortion committee and the stupid men who thought that up. How dumb it was. And how powerful he must feel denying women abortions. I made reference to the poor woman whose husband had just died of cancer but Pearce wouldn't let her get an abortion without his death-bed signature. I told him he only cared about power, his power, and he enjoyed hurting people. I said he was the sickest, most perverse psychopathic diseased excuse of a human I had ever met. And after I finished raging at him, I thanked him for helping me to grow into the powerful woman I had become. Because of his hideousness, I had to develop into the antithesis of his ugliness. And I did.

I couldn't believe the vitriol that poured out of me, and the thoughts that I was having. Finally, he was taking up so much of my psychic space, that I thought I had to do something to stop this. So I did. First, I burned the letter without sending it to him. Then, I had a good long talk with myself and decided that if I ever had a chance to kill him and not go to jail, I would take it, but in the meantime, I was not going to give over my life to this psychopath. And slowly, slowly, I learned to ignore him and the heinous things he did and tried to live my life without his impositions.

Sophie, there will be many times in your life when, unfortunately, you will have to deal with people whom you don't like and with whom you don't agree. You are the only one who can decide how it will go. If you get very upset, you are giving the power over to that other person. Don't let them win that way. When you think someone has control over you, usually it is you not taking control of the situation. Take control of your own life, your own self, and figure out how you can co-exist in this world with the bad guys. Don't ever let people try to ruin your life.

I was in my seventies by the time I came to the realization that evil and cruel people do actually exist and cannot be changed into empathetic humans. I knew about sociopaths and psychopaths, things like *schadenfreude*, but pure evil is very different. Just as we derive great pleasure from giving and sharing and enjoying people's happiness, so do these people derive their pleasure from seeing people suffer, from hurting other people, from denying happiness and from inflicting pain. I don't know why such people exist, but I do know they are here. I have met some myself, read of others in books. It's almost impossible to comprehend that a human being can derive pleasure out of another's suffering, but I've seen it. Literature is full of people like that, throughout all the ages, which must mean the authors have had some experience with this type of person. I hope you do not come across such a person in your life. At best, perhaps read about such a one in great literature. If you should be unfortunate enough to come across such a person, for your own safety and peace of mind, have as little to do with them as possible. I wasted a lot of psychic energy fighting Keith Pearce in my mind and heart, energy that could have been better used to help other people or myself.

1979
Fifth Year of Medical Practice

DOCTORS HAVE TO get continuing education credits to maintain our licenses. One of the ways to get these credits is by participating at medical conferences. Once I was in private practice, I started thinking more about the relationship between doctors and patients. I wrote a medical paper called "The Power Differential Between Doctors and Patients" and applied to present it at a national family practice conference in Ottawa. I was very pleased when it was accepted, since it was coming from the "new breed" of doctors. In it, I wrote about how things like wearing a white coat, sitting across the desk from patients, meeting patients for the first time when they were unclothed (and you weren't), and many other examples, all led to the patient feeling vulnerable in the presence of a powerful doctor. Using medical words without explaining them also changed the power differential. Why would I want to say epistaxis if I could just talk to the patient about a nose bleed? I concluded that such things meant patients weren't getting the best kind of health care available. I was proud of this paper and felt that, while it pointed out the obvious, maybe some hadn't thought about such things before or needed reminding.

I went off to Ottawa for the conference. I thought I delivered my paper quite well and was therefore surprised by the hostile questioning after.

"Why would we want to take off our white coats?" one irate doctor asked. "How would anyone identify us as doctors?"

"My point exactly," I answered politely and explained again about vulnerability.

"I don't have time to see my patients with their clothes on," another doctor angrily shouted at me. "I'm simply too busy."

Another doctor stood up. "Ignore her, she's just a girl. And a flake." His exasperation was clear.

After question period, I gathered my belongings and was on my way to my room to think about things when I was approached by two doctors who introduced themselves as Ben and Jock.

"That was a great paper," Jock said. "We agree with everything you said."

"Yes, that's true," Ben chimed in. "But you need to be able to shut out the others when they get angry with you. These issues are challenging to some of the older doctors, but we are right about them."

"Take heart," Jock said. "Don't get discouraged."

After chatting with Ben and Jock, I felt much better about my presentation and about how it was received by at least a few, if not by many. I really liked those two. In fact, we became good friends and saw each other often for many years.

"MARIA, I WOULD like you to see one my patients, please. His name is John."

Maria looked up from her desk. We often shared patients.

"He's thirty-three years old," I continued. "Married, two kids; I delivered the second one. His wife is very nice. John works for the railway, is bright, reads a lot, smokes a lot of dope, and wants to kill himself." I sighed. "I just don't know what to do with him. I've been talking with him for the past several months and getting nowhere. Will you see him?"

Maria nodded, and John started seeing her on a regular basis. Mandy, his wife, and his two children saw me on a regular basis as well. I liked this family a lot. But Mandy was worried about her husband. I was too. No matter what Maria or I did or said, John was still pretty insistent that he wanted to die. He admitted he loved Mandy and the kids, but said he couldn't find a reason for living.

Maria and I talked about him often. I sent him to a psychiatrist and another physician, just to make sure that we weren't missing anything or not doing something that would help him. We very much wanted him to feel better. John was very amenable to our referrals and good-naturedly went to these consultations but always came back to our office, saying he liked us better.

One morning, after we had been seeing John for about a year, a tearful Mandy came into the office and handed Marlene a letter.

"This is for Ruth and Maria," she said. "It's from John." She burst into tears.

Maria and I looked at the letter together.

"Dear Ruth and Maria," we read, "Please do not feel badly. I have to do this. There is no other way. I know you two tried very hard to help me and I thank you for that. You are both very good but there is nothing that can stop me from doing this. I just want to thank you for everything and tell you how much I apprecia . . ."

The writing slid off the page as John slid out of the world.

He wrote the letter to us from inside his car. I will never forget that letter, the writing slanting to the lower right, more and more, until it stopped as John succumbed to the carbon monoxide he had rigged up in his garage.

"He died two days ago," Mandy was telling Marlene. "The kids and I will miss him. I know he did what he thought was right, but still . . ."

John's death hit us both very hard. I couldn't understand then, and I still don't understand how someone could think that dying was the "right" thing to do in any circumstance. Over forty years later, I am still haunted by the image of John's sad smile, saying he just had to die. I will never understand that.

What I learned is that some times, no matter how hard you try, you cannot influence what will happen. In these circumstances, Sophie, you need to accept things. You can only do the best you can do. If you can't accomplish what you want, it may be time to accept the situation. Of course, you should try as hard as you can to accomplish something. You should. But if you believe you've done all you can do, and still haven't accomplished your goals, it may be time for acceptance.

MARIA AND I also shared another patient, a woman named Jan. She was a brilliant musician, who played with symphony orchestras and made recordings with small ensembles. She was also a brilliant schizophrenic and could fool most people who never suspected she was mentally ill. I liked Jan a lot and tried to be the best possible family physician for her. I liked her a little less after she started calling our home during the night. Usually I answered the telephone when it rang at night since I was often on call.

One night at three a.m., the phone rang, waking both of us from a sound sleep.

"Are you on call tonight?" Maria rolled over in the bed.

"Not as far as I know." I reached for the phone.

"Hello. Dr. Simkin here."

"Hi, Ruth. It's Jan. Can I please speak to Maria?"

"Jan—it's three in the morning! Maria is not available for phone calls."

"No, it's important, I need to speak to her *now*. It's an emergency."

Jan spoke so loudly that Maria could hear the whole conversation. I could tell that Jan was going into a psychotic phase.

I looked at Maria who indicated I should give her the phone.

"Jan," Maria said very firmly, "I cannot talk with you right now. I will see you tomorrow in the office at four p.m. Good night." And she hung up the phone.

"Good job," I said as we both nestled down and tried to get back to sleep.

Within minutes, the phone rang again.

"Hello. Dr. Simkin here."

"Ruth, I need to speak to Maria."

"Maria is not available, Jan. She will see you tomorrow. Please don't call again. I need the phone to be free for medical calls."

"But I need to speak to her."

"Good night, Jan." I hung up the phone.

Within three minutes, the phone rang again.

"Hello. Dr. Simkin here."

"Ruth, I need to speak with Maria."

"Jan, for heaven's sake, you have to stop calling. I need this phone line to be free for medical calls. If you don't stop calling, Maria will be too tired to see you tomorrow. Okay? If you want to see her, then don't call back. Good night."

Ten minutes later, the phone rang again.

"Oh no. Is that who I think it is?"

"Just give me the phone," Maria said and got out of bed.

I pulled the covers up just as I heard her saying, "Jan, I will only see you tomorrow if you let me get some sleep tonight. No more phone calls please." She came back to bed.

"What do you think? Think she'll call again?"

Maria smiled sadly. "I think she went off all her anti-psychotic meds. Hope she makes it until her four p.m. appointment."

I didn't sleep well after that, expecting the phone to ring again. But it didn't.

The next morning, I was in my office, doing chart work—remember, in those days there were no computers in doctors' offices. In fact, I went through medical school and ran my medical practice with no computers or cell phones at all. That was the norm in those days. To tell you the truth, Sophie, I liked the old ways better. We seemed much more involved when we had to write things out by hand.

Marlene poked her head in the doorway.

"Ruth, I just got a phone call from the manager at Jan's apartment building. Apparently, she threw her T.V. out the window."

"Oy," was my response. "Is she okay? Was anyone hurt?"

"I don't think so," Marlene answered.

I sighed. "Where is she now?"

"He doesn't know. He thinks she left."

Just then there was a terrific racket in the waiting room. Marlene went to see what it was. I was not far behind.

And there was Jan—what an imposing figure. She was dressed in business attire. In fact, she looked quite good. But she had taken a shoe off and was banging it on Marlene's desk.

"Jan, what the hell are you doing? Why are you even here?"

"I'm here to see Maria," she answered as though it were obvious.

"Jan, for Pete's sake, it's barely noon. Your appointment with Maria is at four p.m. She's not even here. She won't be here until four."

"I'm here to see Maria," Jan yelled.

"Call the police," I said quietly to Marlene. I knew we would need help subduing her and getting her to hospital. Besides being very agitated and decidedly overwrought, Jan was a very large woman, at least six inches taller than I, and a couple hundred pounds heavier.

"Jan, would you like to come down to my office?" I asked.

"No. My appointment is with Maria."

"Jan, it's eleven-thirty in the morning. Your appointment with Maria isn't until four o'clock."

"I'll wait here." She had a purse in her lap and seemed to calm down a bit. She sat in a chair in the waiting room and I sat down beside her.

I looked at Jan, not quite sure of the next move.

I stayed in the waiting room while Jan began to throw magazines around and upset a table. She couldn't sit still for very long at all. Very quickly two police arrived, a man and a woman.

"Hi, officers," Marlene greeted them.

"We heard you had a problem here. Is that right?"

"Officer, I'm Dr. Simkin," I started, but Jan jumped right up and said, "She's not the doctor, officer, I am. Look at her. Surely you don't believe she is a doctor."

Jan pointed to my feet. "Look. She doesn't even have shoes on. Real doctors don't dress like that. I am the doctor."

The two officers came behind me and each took an arm and held it behind my back. I started laughing. "Marlene, tell them who I am."

"Don't believe that one," Jan was saying, as the two officers started propelling me toward the door. "She's no better."

At this point, I would like to explain how that could be so believable. Jan was dressed in a very elegant rust coloured suit, with dress shoes and jewellery, looking very classy. I, on the other hand, wore jeans, no shoes (I never wore shoes because how would folks be able to appreciate all my wonderful kinky socks!) and a blue Ft. McMurray T-shirt. Dressed as I was, it was quite understandable that the police would think that I was the patient.

As we approached the door, I yelled, "Marlene. C'mon. This is not funny anymore." Except that both Marlene and I were still laughing.

The police almost had me out the door before Marlene could stop laughing long enough to inform them that I was, indeed, Dr. Simkin and that the well-dressed woman over there was the psychotic patient. The police weren't sure whom to believe and Jan had another go at trying to convince them I was their person.

"Look at her, officer. She's not even wearing shoes. Do you think that is a *real* doctor?"

I guess they didn't because we were almost out the door again. Finally Marlene could control her laughter long enough to talk to the police.

"Don't listen to her!" Jan shouted. "She was blonde just a few minutes ago. Her hair was yellow." Since Marlene has the blackest hair I've ever seen and it has always been thus, I think the police started to reassess the situation and they lessened their grip on me as they looked at Jan anew.

"Look, I really am the doctor," I said softly. "This woman is a schizophrenic who is off her meds and waiting to see my partner who is a psychologist. She needs to be admitted to hospital until her medications can be adjusted."

Marlene nodded.

Jan kept shouting, "I am the doctor! I am the doctor!"

"You're going to have to take her to emergency at Foothills Hospital. I'll call to let them know she's on her way."

"Sorry, doctor," the policewoman said. "We thought . . ."

"That's okay. Just take good care of her. Be gentle, but be careful. She's a strong woman."

As soon as the door closed behind them, we burst out laughing again.

Marlene and I straightened up the waiting room, amidst bursts of hysterical laughter at the thought that I almost ended up a patient on the psych ward. Wouldn't have been the first time.

When Maria arrived later that day, Marlene could hardly wait to tell her that I had almost been dragged off by the police. I heard the two of them laughing as I was seeing my patients.

1980
Sixth Year of Medical Practice

ONE OF THE reasons I liked working so much is that we laughed a lot. A very lot. Sometimes things were sad, sometimes things were difficult, but often things were funny.

When I moved into my new offices, after I left Barrie and Gregg, I wanted to decorate it in ways that were a bit, well, different.

One day, my friend Roxy came to see me for an examination. I asked her to change and lie down on the examining table and left the room for just a minute.

Suddenly, I heard an ear-splitting scream. Marlene and I ran into the room.

Roxy was sitting on the table with her head down, looking at the floor. She was still screaming.

"Roxy, what's the matter?" I had no idea what had frightened her so.

"There's a man looking at me," she screamed, wrapping the paper gown tighter around her.

"What? Where?"

"There." Still looking down at the floor, she pointed one finger up toward the ceiling.

Marlene and I burst out laughing.

"Roxy, look. It's not a man. It's a stupid poster."

Okay, I admit that it was pretty strange, but I had a poster of a weird man looking down at the examining table. In the poster, he was lying down and appeared to be looking at whomever was on the examining table. I had just put it up that morning and then promptly forgot about it.

After we all had a good laugh, Marlene and I more than Roxy, Marlene stood at the door, preparing to get back to business.

"Ruth, when you are done with Roxy, there's a detail man waiting to see you."

"What's a detail man?" Roxy asked, distracted but still anxious.

"A detail man," I explained, "is a person from a pharmaceutical company who comes to doctors' offices trying to get us to use their products. Sometimes I learn a bit about the drugs, but I often get free samples, which I can give to my patients to save them some money."

"Oh." Roxy tentatively lay down, still not quite sure about the man on the ceiling looking down on her. I have to admit that he was sort of creepy—a cross between Hannibal Lecter and Pee Wee Herman.

After Roxy's experience, I never forgot to mention to future patients that there was a poster of a man on the ceiling. Virtually everyone else who saw it laughed, thinking it was perfectly placed. Roxy—well, not so much.

After I said good-bye to Roxy, I turned my attention to the detail man.

"What are you detailing today?" I asked the young man in the blue suit and tie and large briefcase.

"Hello, Doctor. We have a new product for you today. I have here," he smiled, "a very special feminine spray deodorant to keep feminine odours at bay."

I did not invite him into my office. The waiting room was now empty so he put several samples of this spray on Marlene's desk.

I listened very patiently as he described why women needed a feminine spray deodorant, and how it kept feminine odours at bay. Truthfully, I don't even know what that means. He smiled at me, then at Marlene. Neither one of us echoed his smile. Nevertheless, he continued talking to our two blank faces for a few minutes, telling us about the importance of his product.

"What do you have for men's smelly balls?" I asked.

'I beg your pardon, what . . . ?" He was a bit flustered.

"Until your company gets and starts marketing that product," I continued, "don't be comin' round here with stuff like that which we don't need."

I don't believe we ever saw that man again.

We laughed about that for years.

MARIA AND I were in the kitchen getting ready for another dinner party. Both of us loved to cook and we entertained a lot. I loved those times at our homes: excellent food, intelligent conversations, lots of laughter. We would, on occasion, have the mayor for dinner, or provincial and federal politicians.

Usually our guests were people who were somehow active in politics and we had some dynamic discussions.

"What are we going to do about the house?" Maria asked.

"The house? What do you mean?"

"Do you think the front hall will be okay?"

I started to chuckle. Wayne and I had done it again. The first time we converted the house, we turned it into a space station flying through outer space. When people walked through the front door, they found themselves in outer space, space ships flying around, planets orbiting, the odd alien around. This time we turned the entry hall and part of the house into a winter wonderland. Everywhere was pretend snow and our guests had to walk through tunnels of it and pass by polar bears and other non-threatening stuffed animals laying atop huge snow mounds to get into the main part of the house. There were angel hair clouds on the ceiling with Christmas lights in them. It really was gorgeous.

"Maria, everyone loves the winter wonderland. Why are you worried? It will be better than okay, right?"

She nodded and smiled.

Maria actually loved it, in fact, loved it more than the space station which she also adored. But at times she worried that we were perhaps too outrageous. I never did. The more outrageous, the better. Everyone who walked through that door immediately laughed and started to play with the stuffed animals, the tunnels, the snow mounds. Wayne and I had totally transformed that part of the house and I was so pleased with it. We kept it up for about six weeks, and then, in January, dismantled the whole thing and the house returned to normal. But those times of decorating and changing the whole character of the house were really special. Not one person who entered didn't stop to play with something in the winter wonderland. Everyone enjoyed it.

So the lesson here, Sophie, is to remember to have fun. Even when you are in the middle of important, heavy projects, or especially then, remember to have fun. Sometimes people forget about that. I always loved to play and had many dress-up parties, like the 50s dance, the African Safari party, and many more. We always laughed a lot and enjoyed ourselves and I hope you can do that as well. Don't ever forget to have fun. It is a very important aspect of our lives.

DURING THE WINTER, Barb, a good friend of Maria's, visited us from Vancouver. She had her two-month old son with her. We had rented a crib and set up her room so she had everything she needed. She was going to stay with us for a week or so and visit her many friends from when she used to live in Calgary. I had met Barb over the years, and felt very comfortable with her staying at the house while Maria and I were at work.

I was particularly busy those days, getting up early to go to work and coming home late. A few days after Barb arrived, Maria stuck her head in my office.

"I'm running home for a bit. Something is wrong with Barb."

"What? What's wrong with her?"

"I'm not sure, but she sounds strange on the phone, says she doesn't feel well, is dizzy, and is worried about the baby."

"Well, okay, call if you need me."

"I will. Bye."

I went back to work and didn't think about it again.

When I got home hours later, Maria came quickly to the door and, with a smile, indicated that I should quietly follow her to our bedroom.

She closed the door.

"What's up? How's Barb?"

"Barb is sleeping now. So is the baby. I don't want to wake them."

"Um, okay, but do we have to sit in the bedroom?"

"No, I just want to tell you what happened."

I stretched out on the bed, exhausted after a long day, put my arms under my head, and said, "Okay, so what gives?"

"Well, I came home. Barb was lying in bed, saying she was quite dizzy. I asked her if she had eaten or drunk anything at all, and she said no. I asked her a lot of questions. I was worried, you know, because she's breastfeeding. I was just about to call you, when she said, 'Well, maybe I did eat something today. Maybe I ate one of Ruth's rum balls. It had an A on it. I thought that was strange, but I ate it anyway. It was very good.'"

"Maybe? Oh my, an A rum ball." I started to laugh, but underneath I felt myself getting a bit sick: sick with concern and anger at myself.

Now, Sophie, an explanation is in order. In the late 1970s and early 80s, it's true, I ate a fair bit of cooked marijuana in those days. And I had a very high drug tolerance. I didn't much like smoking marijuana, but found the perfect way to ingest it in rum balls. I made them in three different strengths: C for beginners, B for people who were used to being stoned, and A for the very few people like me with an extremely high tolerance. Each rum ball was wrapped up tightly in saran wrap, and over the saran wrap sealing it was a big piece of masking tape with either an A, B, or C on it. Each of these individually wrapped balls were then well covered up inside a cookie tin which had tape going all around and over it and on top of the tape was another big piece which said DO NOT TOUCH. This tin was then hidden in my freezer. It never occurred to me that someone would have taken one under those circumstances, particularly an A. I thought they would be safe there, especially since we always had lots of good food in our fridge. Nevertheless, Barb had decided to forego all the delectable comestibles in the fridge and dug around in the freezer to find and unseal my tin, which she opened by ripping through tons of tape under the DO NOT TOUCH sign. She moved all the rum balls around until she came to an A, broke its seal of tape, unwrapped all the saran and ate it. Not only was she not in the A category, she probably would have been intensely stoned on a C rum ball. She never did drugs, and she was breastfeeding at the time.

"How's the baby?" I asked, because that was whom I was worried about.

"He seems fine," Maria answered. "Sleeping a lot. I told Barb what the rum ball was. I don't know why she went for them. They were well marked—I saw what you put into the freezer. And there is so much good stuff in the fridge." She shook her head.

"Look, I'd best check them both as soon as possible."

"Okay, I'll go see if either one is awake."

Five minutes later, Maria came back to the room to say that Barb didn't think she could go out that night and had asked Maria to cancel her date. It was pretty obvious she had to cancel since she was unable to stand up on her own. I went in to see her and the baby.

Other than being very stoned, she was fine. When the baby woke up, he was fine too, although a little sleepy. I told Barb that it would just have to wear off. The thing about eating marijuana as opposed to smoking it, is that it lasts much longer. That's the advantage of eating it for folks like me, but a distinct disadvantage for folks like Barb.

"Barb, you're just going to have to sleep it off. It will take a while. You and your son are just fine. But the next time you see something that says DO NOT TOUCH, you should probably believe it and leave it alone. The warning is there for a reason."

Barb nodded. "Thanks, Ruth. I'm sorry, I'm really sorry."

"It's okay. No harm done. I'm just sorry you've wasted a whole day of your time in Calgary."

Barb's head fell back on her pillow and soon she was sleeping again. We changed and fed the baby and put him back into his crib. And soon he too was sleeping again.

"Easy houseguests." I smiled at Maria.

I guess the lesson here is just because we have a DO NOT TOUCH sign on some of our possessions, it doesn't necessarily mean that people won't. Touch, that is. Eat—well, that's another matter. The important thing here to recognize, Sophie, is that very clear directions about something, anything, do not necessarily mean that people will follow them. We can't assume that just because we are clear, that other people will understand us.

Barb was stoned for two full days. She canceled her date for the following evening, because she still couldn't get out of bed, much less walk and talk coherently. Maria and I took care of the baby. And I stopped keeping rum balls in my freezer. Not only that, but I stopped having marijuana or any other drugs in the house. Although there was no real harm done, I had realized that we were all extremely lucky; we had escaped a potentially disastrous outcome. I thought of possible alternate consequences and was so relieved and grateful that we did not have to deal with them. I would have been responsible and that would have been devastating. I never wanted to be in a position like that again, so my drug-taking days were sufficiently altered from that day forward.

I suppose I should say something about drugs, Sophie, since marijuana, at least, enters into my stories about the 70s when I did use a lot of marijuana. Or pot. Or grass. Or weed. Or whatever you want to call it. In those days, we called it pot, mostly.

Now, some forty years later, I had medical marijuana available to me legally, before marijuana became legal in Canada, and I really didn't want it. I tried it only once when my doctor suggested I do so. I don't like being stoned at all now. I'd much rather have control of my faculties. The irony is that recreational marijuana use has now become legal in Canada at a time I hope I never use it again.

I remember a patient we saw in the first month of medical school, an eighteen-year-old male, and a very heavy marijuana smoker. We were told he used to be quite bright and a star student. He sat on a chair facing us, and when he tried to answer our questions, I don't remember his saying even one complete sentence. His brain had turned to mush. At the time, my fellow pot-smoking students and I all assumed it had nothing to do with the drugs. Today, I believe that we were wrong.

You will do what you need to do when you are growing up. I don't think that anything I say will make a difference. But it might be helpful for you to know that I wish the universe never made marijuana or any other street drugs. They have brought people comfort and pleasure to be sure but they have also caused a lot of trouble and heartache in the world and it's not worth it. In retrospect, I'm sorry that I used drugs like marijuana in the 70s, but the fact is that I did. I hope you are smarter than I was, and think things through more thoroughly than I did.

1981
Seventh Year of Medical Practice

ONE MORNING, I walked into the examining room to see a new patient. "Good morning. What can I do for you today?" I asked the young woman with stringy blonde hair hanging down over her shoulders. She wore a floral print dress with a sweater that had a hole below the right elbow. Her big boots were unlaced over heavy socks.

"I have a punkule on my virginia," she informed me.

I held up my finger. "Just one sec—excuse me—I'll be right back." I quickly got up, quietly shut the door behind me, briskly walked into my office, and closed the door.

Within a few minutes, Marlene opened the door.

"Ruth, are you okay?" I was curled up, lying on the floor with my back to the door. She quickly came over and touched my shoulder. When she saw the tears rolling down my face, she understood that I was laughing.

"Are you quite done?" Marlene asked.

"'A punkule on her virginia,' she said," I got out in between stifled guffaws. "Oh lordy me, a punkule." I rolled on the floor with laughter.

Marlene knelt beside me and we both laughed for a minute. Shortly, we got up, I took a deep breath before I went back into the examining room, hoping I got all the laughter out of me for a while. As funny as some things were, I never wanted to embarrass my patients or ever make them feel uncomfortable.

One never knew who was waiting on the other side of that door. Marlene always made me look good, by telling me what I had to know before I walked into the room.

"Ruth, it's a new guy, Jacques. I'm not sure what he wants—something about his leg."

"Okay, thanks. I guess I'll find out." I walked into the examining room and saw a very thin, middle aged man sitting straight up in the chair. He wore a plaid shirt, buttoned up to the neck and tucked neatly into blue jeans with a brown belt.

"Hello, Jacques. What can I do for you today?"

"My mudder, she 'ad de leg, eh? And den dey 'ad to cut it off."

I sat across from him, nodding, but not quite knowing why he was there or what the problem was.

I was always fascinated by people and could watch and listen to them forever. At times, it took me a bit longer to figure out why they were there and how I could help them. Jacques was reassured, after doing appropriate blood tests, that he did not have diabetes like his mother and was not likely to lose his leg.

MARLENE KNOCKED ON the door.

"Ruth, Windi is on the phone for you. He says it's urgent."

Windi Earthworm was one of my more interesting patients. He was a street social worker, hanging out on the 8th Ave. Mall, wearing his long denim skirt, his hair often tied back into a pony-tail. He would pick up kids who had nowhere to go and take care of them. Things were different back then. Windi's heart was in the right place, for sure, and I know he helped a lot of people. But he was a little peculiar. I guess I was, too, and that's why we liked each other.

I picked up the phone.

"Hi, Windi. What's up?"

"I just sent Michael to the hospital," he said quickly. "I told them he was your patient. You should be hearing from them pretty soon."

"Aw, Windi, c'mon. You know I don't have room for more patients. I'm really busy these days."

"Ruth, he's all alone. He's from Quebec. He needs to be in hospital and I think you can help him. Please."

"Okay, Windi, but no more. I can only work twenty-seven hours a day."

He laughed. "Thanks. See ya."

Not two minutes passed before the hospital called.

"Dr. Simkin, we have a patient of yours here. He's in a psychotic state. We're sending him up to the psych ward."

"Thanks. I know about him. I'll be there within the hour to see him."

I drove to the hospital to meet Michael from Quebec. That, and the fact he was psychotic, was all I knew about him.

When I arrived on the psych ward, two nurses ran up to me.

"He's here, but we don't know what to do with him. Most of the staff are afraid to approach him."

"Why? Where is he?"

The nurses pointed to a young man. He was walking in slow motion as though he were on the moon with no gravity, both arms held out to the sides, legs bent at the knee and lifted high with each step. He was tall, thin, with dark hair that fell in curls over his forehead. I thought he was very good looking, albeit not entirely *compos mentis*. I walked up right behind him and started imitating him, walking just like he was walking: arms held out, legs lifted high in the air. After a few more moon steps, I said, "Would you like to come onto my space ship?"

"Sure," he answered. I turned around and he followed me, both of us moon walking slowly, arms out, legs high, right into his room. The nurses watched us, mouths agape, as they couldn't believe what we were doing—well, what I was doing. We got inside his room and then we sat down on his bed.

"Now, what's the problem?"

And we talked.

Michael had a drug-induced psychosis. He was in hospital for three days, then discharged. A couple of months later, I got a postcard from Quebec. It said, "Thank you for all your help in Calgary. Everything is fine now. I am back in university. Michael."

"Thank you, Windi." I smiled.

I PARTICULARLY LIKED one of my patients, Jodie, who was head of the then-called Battered Women's Organization, a group with whom I had done some work. They offered counselling and helped women leave destructive households. Jodie was intelligent, had a great sense of humour, and seemed open and honest about all things. We often talked about battered women and the problems they faced. I knew from being active in the women's community that her reputation in the field was stellar.

After being her physician for three or four years, I went into the examining room to see Jodie. I sat down and we talked as we usually did (Marlene always knew which patients she should book for a longer time). I noticed Jodie wasn't quite her customary jovial self.

"Jodie, what's up? Something bothering you?"

She shook her head, but she kept her head down, something very unusual.

"Jodie, c'mon, what's up? What's happening here?"

And then, like a blast, I got it. Jodie was a battered woman herself.

"How long has it been going on?"

She looked up at me. "Years. Many years."

"Do you have any injuries now?"

"Just the normal bruises. But he's smart. Usually, they're where you can't see them. He needs me to keep working."

I nodded and sat there in silence.

"Oh, Ruth, I'm so embarrassed." She started sobbing.

"Jodie, there is no need to be embarrassed. None at all. It's okay. It really is. Let's talk about what we need to do now."

And we did. We got her out of that relationship, quietly, while she kept her job. She went into therapy to help her readjust. I kept seeing her for many more years.

The lesson here, Sophie, is not to always assume we know everything we think we do. I saw this woman for years without suspecting she was a battered woman and I was better than most at figuring these things out. We need to be open and accepting and provide people with a safe place to tell us what they need to say.

MARLENE WAS STANDING at my door.

"Linda just called. She told me she had a very bad headache, so I fitted her in this morning."

"Great, Marlene, thanks."

Marlene knew that I would always see patients with a problem. I would never tell anyone to take two aspirins and go to bed. If they felt they needed to call me, then I would see them.

I liked Linda. Her husband was also my patient and I had delivered their children.

I was truly their family doctor. She was in her thirties and not one to exaggerate medical problems so when I saw her an hour later, something did not seem right.

"My head is sore, Ruth, right here." She pointed toward the back of her head. This did not seem like an ordinary headache.

"You know, Linda, I would like you to go to the hospital for some tests. Just to be sure, you understand. I want to make sure we are not dealing with anything here that needs attention and, if we are, well, then, we'll do what we have to do."

Somehow, I just knew she was having a cranial bleed.

I sent her straight to emergency and called them to explain the situation.

A few hours later, I got a phone call from the neurosurgeon.

"Ruth, hi. Claude LeBlanc here. We're taking your patient up to the OR right now. She has a cranial bleed. Good call. If you hadn't sent her in this morning, I don't think she would have made it. As it is, we'll see what we can do. Hopefully, she will be fine after the surgery."

Linda was in the hospital for many weeks, unable to move her head at all because of the sandbags all around her on the bed. She had to keep her head very still for a time post-operatively. But ultimately she was discharged with relatively little neurological deficit.

When she came to my office a few weeks after she got out of hospital, she hopped up on the examining table.

"Thanks for saving my life, Ruth."

"Oh, I didn't save your life, Linda. You were a great patient under very difficult circumstances. I'm just delighted that everything worked out so well."

"Okay. But thanks." She smiled.

"You're welcome." I smiled back.

That was one of the few times where I knew I had really made a difference. I realize that many people may not have seen her so quickly, nor diagnosed her correctly in the office, nor sent her off to the hospital to see a neurosurgeon like I did. I felt good.

One lesson here, Sophie, is that it is a good idea to believe people and to give them the benefit of the doubt. And going along with that is trusting your own instincts. Believe not only others but yourself as well.

When I had decided that I wanted to be a doctor, I wanted to be like Drs. Doupe and Brennecke, both of whom I believed had saved my life. Both of them were incredibly fine physicians: they believed their patients, they acted on what their patients said and did right by them. When I diagnosed Linda, even though neither Dr. Doupe nor Dr. Brennecke were living, I felt as though I had made them proud. And me too. I was proud of me. Remember, Sophie— it's okay to be proud of yourself when you do something that deserves feeling proud. Nothing wrong with that at all.

Something else happened in 1981 that made me proud. In 1980, the YWCA had instituted the Women of the Year awards. These were started in honour and celebration of the fact that it had been fifty years since women were recognized as "Persons" by the Privy Council of Great Britain and that became law. This was a huge thing. It meant that women had rights and could vote, which had not been the case fifty years earlier.

Maria and I had both been instrumental in helping to get this annual celebration going and, that first year, were both very active in putting on the very first dinner where women received Women of the Year Awards. By the second year, while we were both working on it, we were not as much involved. We had both been asked, individually and jointly, to run for these awards. We discussed it at length and decided we wanted to run together. I was more keen to do this than Maria who wanted more to run individually but, in the end, she was happy to go along with it. There were six different categories for Women of the Year and Maria and I were nominated in three of them: Community Service—Volunteer; Health and Fitness; Public Affairs.

The dinner was a classy affair. Everyone got dressed to the nines and it was wonderful to see hundreds of women so elegantly adorned. My mother flew out to be with us. I could tell how proud she was to be there, just basking in the fact that we had been nominated. I can't explain how wonderful I felt that she was there to celebrate how I had been living my life; it made me feel loved beyond belief.

We did win, in Health and Fitness, and, luckily for us, that year the award was a beautiful sculpture by Katie Ohe, one of my favourite Calgary artists. After that year, winners received a fancy pin. That sculpture now sits on my window ledge and I see it every day and remember . . .

I remember my mother's absolute delight when we won. She ordered a magnum of champagne for our table. She couldn't stop smiling and, because of that, I couldn't stop smiling. For all the years I had caused her such pain, I was thrilled I could now do something that pleased her so much.

And of course, I was pleased too. This was a big deal in our community. It felt good to be recognized.

1982
Eighth Year of Medical Practice

AFTER MARIA GOT her PhD, she decided to go into an office with another psychologist. I also wanted another medical doctor in the office with me as I was working incredibly long hours. I had, after all, built a two-doctor office and wanted another woman physician to come in with me. I figured that the male medical students had chances to go in with other doctors, but female residents and new physicians did not have so many chances. I wanted to be able to do something positive for a new female physician, even though I was still pretty new myself.

After hearing that I was looking for another female physician, Linda arrived. I showed her around, introduced her to Marlene, told her that I wanted a two-doctor office, that I knew most doctors had a hard time in the beginning and so I was wanting to give a female physician a break. The terms were very good. Linda returned with her accountant (a male) and we went through the whole thing again.

Two days later, Linda left a message for me saying she wasn't interested. I later found out that she had indeed wanted to come, but her accountant talked her out of it. He said that there had to be a trick—it was just too good to be true. He couldn't figure out what my game was, or how I was going to somehow cheat her, but he was sure that I would try something because no one makes offers that good for no reason. She believed him. Too bad she couldn't have believed me instead. It did work out well for me though because, as the years went on and I got to know her better, I realized she would not have been the right person for me to have in my office. The absolutely right person showed up shortly after—my partner Dr. Jann Rogers—who was a perfect partner in every way. We had a fantastic practice together. I loved working with Jann. She was smart, kind, funny, loved animals and kids and was a wonderful physician and the ideal partner. We worked very well together.

One day, when I was feeling a bit down, I went in to see my next patient. He was a young man in his thirties, extremely good looking, in jeans, plaid shirt, work boots.

"Hello," I said. "I'm Dr. Simkin."

"I'm Joe. Pete, the bricklayer, sent me to see you. He says you're okay."

That made my day, and my sadness evaporated. I had a very high percentage of women in my practice, but I saw their boyfriends and husbands as well. But when this guy said Pete the bricklayer had sent him, I beamed. I felt I had made it as a physician. Thank you, Pete.

The next patient was a woman who was newly pregnant. I delivered a lot of babies during the first fifteen years of my practice and loved it. When I was taking the history, I asked her about previous pregnancies.

"Yes," she told me, hands sitting over her knees, "I was pregnant before, but I had to have a Serian due to hyplaglycemia."

I smiled and nodded. It was a good thing I studied patient medicalese while in my residency.

Another time I walked into the examination room to check a guy's blood pressure. I had never seen him before. He slipped off his shirt, and there on his arm was a large tattoo that said, "I love pussy." Now this was at the height of my feminist activism and for a brief second, I wasn't sure how to react. I did consider amputating his arm, but then I thought that if I treated him with dignity and respect, it was possible, not probable but still possible, that he would end up treating me, and hopefully others, that way. And so I did. I think he was just passing through Calgary, so I didn't see him again. I don't know if respectful treatment made him respectful in turn, but I know I did the right thing. I don't think it is ever wrong to treat people with dignity and respect.

I saw another patient because he had had a seizure. "They did tests for epilepsy," he told me. "I had a scam 'n' that."

I walked into the next room to see an elderly lady sitting in the chair. She wore a little blue hat with flowers and a veil and a blue dress. Her purse was in her lap.

"Doctor," she started before I had even shut the door, "I had neuritis of the nerves, but the lymph gnomes were clear, so I wasn't maligmant. But I still have the nauseation."

I just loved my patients!

Having my own office allowed me to work in my own way at my own pace. My charting was always very good because of the forms I had designed and they were better than others I'd seen. I always asked patients about sexual and physical abuse and all kinds of other questions that weren't usually asked, and often got surprising responses.

I entered an examining room to do a physical exam on a new patient, a seventy-year-old woman. Before any examination, I always talked to my patients first while they were fully clothed. I liked this woman; she seemed pleasant, intelligent, and gray cells have always had a special appeal for me.

"Have you ever been sexually abused?" I asked, as I always did.

Much to my amazement, she slid down on her chair and started crying.

I offered her some tissue, and sat silently waiting.

"I was raped when I was sixteen." She dried her tears with the tissue. "I have never told anyone until now."

"Why was that?" I asked gently.

"No one ever asked me." She paused. "And I was too ashamed to bring it up."

"Would you like to talk to someone now, to get some closure on this terrible thing that happened to you?"

She slowly nodded.

I referred her to the rape crisis centre and when she returned to see me months later, she had a glow about her and thanked me profusely for helping her finally deal with that terrible episode of her life.

ALTHOUGH I WAS spending a lot of time seeing patients, I was also very involved in the politics of the day. The feminist movement, as it was called in the 70s and 80s, was going strong and there were always many meetings, conferences, and political actions that were happening. We often had luncheon meetings with political people, almost all of whom were men. Every single time we did this, no matter who was hosting the meal, the cheque went to the gentleman. Many of us were getting tired of always seeing women dismissed and ignored in virtually every capacity. So we decided to form our own club. That is how Inter Se, which means "among ourselves," came into being. It was in a new building downtown, right in the center of things. The whole club was quite elegant. We had a very classy dining room and, because we hired a well-known chef, the food was outstanding. One of the first rules we made was that only members could pay bills and only women could be members. So when we invited a politician to lunch, the cheque automatically would come to us. This was a minor thing in the big picture, paying a luncheon bill, but it was so tiring always fighting erroneous assumptions and this gave us a respite.

Inter Se was pretty spectacular. We had incredible parties—costume parties on Halloween, Las Vegas type casino evenings, and once, a Medieval dinner party with wandering minstrels, with my friend Wes and I elaborately dressed as king and queen. We had a long table, with no silverware at all and everyone was expected to eat with their hands. It was messy but fun. For a few years, we used our club all the time. I remember one evening Maria and I unexpectedly got news of some important politician coming from Ottawa and, somehow, the dinner party was going to be at our home that evening. We just called our chef at Inter Se and, after both of us had worked a full day at our offices, we were able to host a very elegant impressive dinner at home.

I remember initially thinking with other women that we should have a place where we could do things the way we wanted, and that was why we started a private club. It was even better than we could have imagined. It reminded me of a time in Winnipeg when I was a young teenager. We had grown up without much of anything and, about this time, my dad and his brothers started to do well with their business, as did many of their cohorts in the city. It was in the days when golfing was becoming the thing, or at least, we were just becoming aware of it. We were Jewish, and none of the golf clubs allowed Jewish members, so the men got together and built their own golf club. We used to go there quite often for dinner. But unlike the golf club, Inter Se eventually ended; I don't really remember why.

So, Sophie, keep these stories in mind. If there is something you need or want and it doesn't exist for you or exist in the way you would like, then make your own. Build it, invent it, start it—no reason why not. Do what needs to be done, and enjoy. Don't hesitate even for a second. Just because something doesn't exist doesn't mean it shouldn't. Bring it into being if it is something you want. Remember my favourite bumper sticker: Enjoy Life. It has an expiration date.

MARLENE CAME INTO the staff room where I was having a quick sandwich between patients. "I was just talking with that nurse from across the hall,"

"Oh yeah?" I looked up from my medical journal. I almost always read when I wasn't seeing patients, so I could keep up with everything medical.

"Yeah. She said the doctor there sees over a hundred patients a day."

"A hundred patients a day. Holy shit. No wonder I don't make any money at this thing. I come to work at seven a.m. after making rounds at the hospital and leave after seven p.m. And I only see thirty patients on a big day."

"I know, Ruth, but she told me that some of the patients don't even spend one full minute with him. Most of them come for prescriptions."

"Yeah, I heard he's the one to go to if you want some drugs. I would never do that. Besides, I like how I practice medicine. I just wish I could make a living at it."

You know, Sophie, for all the many years I had my own practice, I never made much money at it until I went on salary at a clinic. I paid my staff higher than minimum wages with all the benefits, I designed and printed my own charts that were consistent with my practice, and I spent time and had a relationship with every single one of my patients. I was fortunate to have some family income from which I could live but I went through that quickly. I never regretted how I practiced medicine, I only regretted that there were not many (if any) like me. I felt very certain I was doing a good thing. Better still, all my patients felt that, too. They were loyal and devoted and, to this day, I still get letters and emails from people I saw many decades ago, telling me how much I had helped them. The doctor from across the hall is probably somewhere on the French Riviera, in a first-class hotel, with buckets of money to spend. I don't believe he helped many of the people he saw.

I considered reporting him once when I heard he had done something dangerous to a patient. After careful consideration, I decided to stay out of it completely. I was reluctant to act upon rumour and concrete facts were unavailable. I'm not sure that was the right thing to do; it was all hearsay anyway.

Sophie, even if you are the only one doing things your way, if you think it's the right way, then don't stop. You will regret it if you compromise your own values and judgements. Do what you think is right. If you are the only one, make sure it is right and continue.

I SAW A lot of patients from the University of Calgary. Judy was a professor, brilliant, and more than just a little strange. Unfortunately, she developed a cancer in her eye. It was fortunate that I caught it, but unfortunate that she had to have it in the first place. It was highly virulent, and the specialist did not give her more than another few months to live. The cancer had already spread and, with all the metastases, she was feeling poorly by the time I first saw her. She continued to work at the university as long as she could. She was a few years older than I, unmarried, and a committed academic. I tried to get as much information about her as possible, through her and her friends at the University, so I could give her the best possible care.

One day she was in my office.

"Do you have any siblings?" I asked.

"No. No siblings."

"Are your parents alive?"

"Yes." She did not tend to volunteer much information. I was going to have to work at it.

"Where do they live?"

"Boston."

"Do they ever come here to visit?"

"No."

"Do they know about your disease?"

"No." Silence.

"Do you not think you should tell them?"

"No."

"Look, Judy, I know this is difficult, but do you not think it is unfair not to let them know what is going on with you? You will be in the hospital soon and you might want someone to be with you."

"Not them."

"Is there anybody else then that you might want to be with you?"

"No."

"Have you and your parents fought about something?"

"No."

"Can you tell me why you don't want them to know or to come here?"

"No."

Since she was my patient and her parents were not, I had to respect her wishes. I couldn't understand this attitude though. I have always been quite close to my family, even when we were fighting. It didn't make sense to me at all.

A week went by and she returned. Again I asked about her parents. Again she declined to talk to them or see them. I asked her about them every time she came in.

One of those times, I asked as usual, "Have you spoken to your parents?"

"No."

"Would you like me to speak with your parents?"

"Do as you wish. I don't care."

"So it's okay with you if I call your parents?"

"If you want." She shrugged.

That evening after I was finished seeing all my patients, I located her parents in Boston. They were both well-known professors at a university. I explained who I was, and why I was calling.

"Oh my, we'll come down immediately," her mother told me.

"Well, I think you need to understand that she has said she doesn't want to see you or talk with you. Do you know what that is about?"

"Not really," her father said. "She went to Calgary and told us she wanted to be independent and hasn't spoken to us since."

"Well, as long as she is okay with my talking to you, I will keep you informed as often as you like."

"Every day if you can please," her mother said, choking back the tears.

A few days later, Judy was admitted to the hospital. She was pretty frail; I think she knew she would not be going home.

"Judy, I spoke with your parents. They really want to come down. They love you a lot and want to be with you. Will you see them?"

"No."

"Judy, what is this about?" I was feeling very frustrated. Her parents seemed really nice on the phone, which of course, might not mean anything. Nevertheless, it was sad, their only child dying in hospital, far away in another country. Of course they would want to be here.

"Why won't you see them?"

Once again, she shrugged and turned away.

When I called her parents that night, they said they were coming anyway. They understood they couldn't see her, but they would be there just in case she would allow them to come into her room. And they were true to their word.

The next day, I got to the ward where Judy was and saw two people who had to be her parents standing in the hallway. I went up to introduce myself.

"We're just waiting here in case she changes her mind," her mother said. "The nurse told her we were here, but she didn't want to see us."

"I'll try." I went into her room.

"Judy, your parents are here. Can they come in to see you?"

"No."

"Judy, you know you are not going to be around much longer. They've travelled here to be with you. They really love you. I think you should let them in."

"No."

And that's the way it was. She died shortly thereafter and her parents got to see her dead body. But they never did see her alive one. That was one of the saddest cases I had. I don't know why it affected me so much—maybe because I am so close to my own family—but seeing the love and respect her parents had for her made her dismissal of them painful to watch. I felt like a failure, although I am not sure what else I could have done. To this day, I have absolutely no idea why she would not see or talk to them.

You know, Sophie, it's difficult to respect people's wishes when we don't agree with them but we still do need to respect them. It's only what I would like for myself in return and I imagine you feel the same way. It's part of being in a civilized society. Life is full of contradictions and tricky things. I think people who do well are those who are able to come to terms with all the contradictions with which we have to deal and be able to somehow make sense of it all, or at least, accept things as they are.

1983
Ninth Year of Medical Practice

I'VE HAD ALL kinds of patients and occasionally had to do WCB or Workers Compensation Board cases. One time, John, a man in his sixties, came to me complaining about his foot that he had injured at work by jumping off a truck. I examined him, did x-rays, told him to take two weeks off and rest it, and filled out the form. As long as I signed the Workers Compensation Board pink form, the patient would get payment. Two weeks later he returned and said it was no better. I could find nothing wrong with him at all but, because it was a WCB case, I gave him the benefit of the doubt and sent him to an orthopaedic surgeon, just in case I missed something. Nope, he couldn't find anything wrong either but John came back saying it was no better, he would still need more time off work. I re-examined him very carefully and sent him to an internist to check out his vascular system. John returned, saying his leg was mighty sore and he just could not go back to work. Two and a half months had gone by since the initial visit. Every time he came to me I examined him carefully, and every time I found absolutely nothing wrong with him. Still, he was so insistent that his leg was sore, I believed him. Why would he lie?

One day I was seeing another patient, Mindy. who came to see me a year earlier with her mother who had been my patient for years. Mindy decided she liked me and wanted me to be her doctor too. I was examining her and casually asked, "How's your mother?"

"Great!" Mindy answered. "Especially since she started dancing a few months ago."

"Dancing?"

"Yes. She goes every week with her new friend, John. I believe he is a patient of yours too. They love to go to this place out of town somewhere."

"I see." I smiled at her.

A few days later, John came in for me to sign his WCB form. I had to do that every two weeks as long as he was off work and receiving compensation.

"Hi, John, how are you doing today?" I asked.

"Oh, not too good, doctor. This leg is just sooo sore."

"I see. Is it just as sore when you go dancing?"

"What?" He sat up quickly.

"Well, don't you go dancing every week?"

"Uh, well, um I guess, uh, look, can you just sign the form?"

"No, John, I can't. I have examined you many times. I have sent you to two different specialists, done x-rays, and nobody can find anything wrong with you. So I don't believe I can sign your WCB forms anymore. I'm sorry. But I hope you continue to enjoy your dancing." I smiled gently at him.

Two weeks later, I received a letter from the College of Physicians and Surgeons of Alberta. John had reported me for malpractice and they were doing a full investigation of me. Now, I knew that I did not do anything wrong but these investigations took forever and they were serious. I had to send them all my chartings and notes, and all the results from the specialists. It took many hours for me to get it all together, spending an entire week-end in the office gathering everything the College wanted. But, at least I had taken meticulous notes.

Although I had done nothing at all unacceptable, I never knew what the College might do. I finally got a letter from the College of Physicians and Surgeons of Alberta absolving me of any wrong-doing. The best part of it was a copy of the letter they sent to John, where they said not only did Dr. Simkin do nothing irregular, but the standard of medical care he received was far above the norm. Of course, nothing was said about the many hours I spent preparing my reports for the college, done on my own time and for which I did not receive a penny.

As the years went by, I gained more confidence and stopped looking over my shoulder in anticipation of being sideswiped by Drs. Satland or Pearce. I even became an Assistant Professor at the University of Calgary Medical School and enjoyed teaching the new medical students. Overall I got very good reviews and I loved teaching them. Well, most of them. Mel was a very tall, handsome by conventional standards, third year medical student who thought he was the ultimate gift to the field of medicine. He would strut around the hospital, stethoscope dangling around his neck, smiling at everyone. While I didn't much like him, I tried to be fair to everybody. Most of the medical students enjoyed working with me, delivering babies and seeing patients. I tended to give them as much responsibility and experience as I thought they could handle and really tried to teach them while being kind at the same time.

One day, I was in the delivery room with Margo, one of my patients, and Mel walked in. He had been assigned to Obstetrics for a few weeks. Margo was having a bit of trouble with the delivery and I was speaking to her quietly and gently, trying to keep her calm. Mel walked around to where I was standing and saw that the baby was starting to crown. Margo was pushing and it would have been better had she not pushed at that point.

"Whoa there, dear," Mel loudly shouted. "Easy does it, honey, whoa there." I looked at him.

He must have thought I approved because he continued. "Whoa there now, easy now."

"Out!" I shouted. "Get out of my delivery room right now. When you can speak to a woman as though she is a person and not a horse, maybe you can come back. For now, get out of here and go to a stable."

I think Mel thought I was joking because his eyes were smiling (he had a mask on, of course).

"Get out right now. Don't you ever come back into my delivery room until you speak respectfully and properly to the patients. Out!"

Mel stared at me in disbelief, eyes not smiling now. He slowly slunk out of the delivery room.

Margo looked at me and silently mouthed, "Thank you."

I was investigated by the College once more while I worked in that office. One morning, Marlene came down the hall to talk with me.

"Ruth, there is a woman on the phone who insists on seeing you."

"But, Marlene, I'm not seeing any new patients. I can only work so many hours in a day."

"I know, and that's what I told her. But she insists. She says you are the only person in the world who can help her. She won't get off the phone."

"Well, okay." I sighed. "I'll see her on two conditions. I'll have to see her for a physical which could take up to an hour, and the only time I have to do it is seven a.m. tomorrow morning. So if she'll come in to see me then, I'll see her. And she will also have to pay the five dollar fee."

"Okay." Marlene went off to talk to the woman.

I spent longer than most doctors doing my physicals, asking a lot more questions and listening a lot more. I started charging five dollars for a physical exam as most other doctors had been doing. I was barely breaking even in this office, even though I was working ten or twelve hours a day. Another reason I added the five dollar fee for this new patient was that, since I was going to come into the office an hour earlier to see her, I wanted to make sure she was serious about seeing me.

When I arrived the next morning to open up, a woman was waiting at the door. I had told Marlene not to come until eight, as usual.

"Hi. You must be Sharon. I'm Dr. Simkin."

"Thank you so much for seeing me, Doctor. I'm so grateful."

"No problem." I unlocked the door and swung it wide open. "C'mon in."

As I had suspected, Sharon had a very complicated history and complicated complaints. I spent a full hour with her and then ordered a lot of tests. I asked her to book another appointment in two weeks and we would go over all the test results then. She thought that was a great plan.

After she left, Marlene came into my office.

"That new patient refused to pay the five dollars. She said she is on welfare and you have no business charging her."

"Yeah, except I came in an hour early to see her and she had already agreed to pay the five dollars. Here's the thing, Marlene. Don't book her for another appointment until she pays the five dollars for this one. It's a one-time charge and she agreed to it. She is breaking her commitment."

"Okay," Marlene said and went back to her desk.

A few days later, Marlene came into my office. "That Sharon gal, the new patient, just called. I told her what you said, about the five dollars. She started yelling at me, telling me she was on welfare and where did I get off charging her. She yelled at me for quite a while."

"I don't want anyone yelling at my nurse. Bring me her number please."

I dialed the number and Sharon answered.

"Hi Sharon. It's Dr. Simkin here."

"Oh, uh, hi." It was clear that she was quite surprised to hear from me.

"Listen, before I agreed to see you, you consented to pay the extra fee of five dollars. That was the commitment between us. I'm perfectly okay if you don't want to pay it, but then I can't see you anymore because you broke your commitment. I'll be happy to send your test results to any doctor you tell me. But I won't be seeing you. And, please, don't call and yell at my nurse any more. We don't like that."

"Well, what are my results?"

"I'm sorry, I don't do results over the phone. Now, if you can give me the name of an alternate doctor, I will be happy to send off your results. If you want to come here to get them, that's fine. But you will have to pay the five dollars first. You let us know what you decide to do."

That was the last I ever heard from Sharon. But not the last I ever heard from The College of Physicians and Surgeons of Alberta. I got a very nasty letter asking how I dared charge a welfare patient.

I wrote back to the College and informed them that their welfare patient had just come back from a two week holiday in Mexico and that she smoked over a package of cigarettes a day. She was perhaps not quite as destitute as she would have one believe. I charged her five dollars because I didn't want to see her given my patient load and wanted to know if she was really serious about being a patient here: obviously, she wasn't. She committed to paying that before we knew she was on welfare and, as far as I was concerned, we had a contract which she refused to honour.

The next letter I got from the College was a bit nicer, but not a whole lot. They said they understood my point but that I was never to charge a welfare patient again. They were not pleased. Nor was I. I thought that Sharon was playing everybody. But I stuck to my guns and refused to see her again, telling her and the College that I would be happy to send her results to any doctor she wanted. She never gave me a name.

Aside from Sharon and John, most of my patients were wonderful. In fact, within a year of opening my own office, many of the movers and shakers of the women's community were my patients. I knew a lot of these women, if not personally, then by reputation. I was a bit puzzled about why they came to me, but they seemed to like coming and always returned. In time, I learned a major lesson from these women, whom others look at and say to themselves or their friends, "How does she do that? How does she hold herself together like that? She is so accomplished, she can do anything! And she is always so present, so smart."

Initially, I asked those questions too and thought of these women as a new breed, different from myself. Yet sooner or later, every one of them would break down in my office, crying about something, saying, "please don't tell anyone about this." They would totally decompensate, something I never thought they would do. And, after we talked, they would dry their tears, refresh their make-up (some of them), and when they went back into the waiting room, everyone would say, "Oh, look! There's so-and-so. How does she always manage to be so on top of things?"

About that time I read a book, *The Imposter Syndrome*, about women who were very successful but felt that they got ahead because of reasons other than their own abilities and that they were really failures. Many highly successful women really feel that they are fooling people, that they are not really as good or talented as people think, that they are imposters. I thought this was a reasonable theory, and it's still out there. I myself used to think that I was an imposter, not really capable of doing what I did, but I don't anymore. I discovered I really was capable and an excellent physician, but it took a long time for me to feel that.

Long before medical school, I thought I was too stupid to ever pass first year chemistry. Dr. B. had me see a psychologist who did intelligence testing on me. I was sure the tests would confirm just how stupid I was. When Dr. Rich was all done with the testing, she asked me what I wanted to study.

I look at her sheepishly and sort of half mumbled, "Well, I kinda wanna be a doctor, but I don't think I'm smart enough to pass first year chemistry."

She smiled warmly at me. "Ruth, you can study anything at all that you want to study. Your IQ is near genius."

I looked up at her, not quite believing the words I heard.

"Really? You really think I can pass first year chemistry?"

"Yes, Ruth, and physics, too, or anything else you might want to do. Don't be afraid to try."

"Really?" I asked again. I was having some trouble integrating this.

"Yes, really." She smiled again. "Good luck with your studies."

And that gave me confidence to study science. I studied chemistry, biological and physical chemistry, nuclear and atomic physics and more and I had a blast. I loved it. I just needed to believe that it was a possibility for me. Once I absorbed what Dr. Rich had told me, I was off and running.

Sophie, I was insecure in those days and needed someone to get me going. If you ever find yourself in that situation, then don't hesitate to get an expert to validate whatever needs verifying for you. I hope you get to know yourself and trust yourself so that you never develop the Imposter Syndrome. Accept your capabilities and be proud of them. Seeing the women in my practice, the high rollers, the successes, who thought they were phonies, taught me a lot about trusting myself and accepting my own abilities. Marlene used to say that I was never afraid to branch out and try different things, that I was never afraid to get out of my comfort zone. I'm proud of that. I hope you become proud of whatever it is you end up doing and enjoy your travels down the road to success.

1984
Tenth Year of Medical Practice

IN 1977, BEFORE the borders were open to individuals, I organized a women's tour group to China. Twenty of us, including my sister and mother, went for one month. Once there, my mother's bursitis became excruciatingly painful and our Chinese guide suggested she try acupuncture. My mother was very keen to try it while I, in my arrogance, ridiculed it. After all, I was a Western-trained physician; how could sticking some needles into a person help? Well, they did. A lot. The acupuncture cured her bursitis completely. I was not fully convinced but did not forget that. After we returned, I became interested in alternative ways to help people and, seven years later, I was on my way back to China, to study at the Shanghai College of Traditional Chinese Medicine, a three month World Health Organization approved course in acupuncture. The course was for physicians, so we already had basic knowledge of anatomy, physiology, and so forth.

Interestingly, Joanne, who had her own family practice across town, did the course with me. This time we travelled as just friends and got along very well. The course was wonderful, difficult, and lots of work, but I loved it. We worked six full days and several nights a week. We sat some very difficult practical, oral, and written exams. I passed and received my WHO diploma in acupuncture. When I returned, I wrote to the College of Physicians and Surgeons of Alberta, stating that I would like to incorporate acupuncture into my practice. And so I came to be the very first physician who practiced acupuncture with the approval of the College. As mentioned, I always liked being the first of something. I found that sometimes Western medicine worked better, sometimes Eastern medicine worked better, depending upon what a particular patient needed. For example, if I was having a cardiac arrest, I would want a very modern Intensive Care Unit with all the bells and whistles. But for chronic joint pain, I would probably do better with acupuncture than Western medicine. I liked having many options.

Shortly after my return from China, I was planning a family visit to your grandmother. Your mother was then in grade three and she asked if I would come to talk to her class about acupuncture. I was delighted to do so and brought my little show and tell box, containing a plastic human model with lines of the Chinese meridians marked on the body, some acupuncture needles, and other things I thought the kids might find interesting. I talked to the class and then the teacher asked if I could do a demonstration. I told her I wasn't comfortable doing it on little kids, and she said, "Oh no, do it on me."

"Are you sure?" I asked.

"Absolutely. What would you like me to do?"

I had her sit in a chair in the middle of the room, and was going to give her acupuncture in a spot just below her knee, which was a great general energy spot, quite innocuous, and people usually felt very energized after having acupuncture there. So I explained what I was doing and put the needle into her leg.

Now, Sophie, in all the decades in which I practiced acupuncture and the hundreds upon hundreds of people I treated, I only ever had two people faint. And your mother's teacher was one of them. She fell to the floor, out cold.

"You killed our teacher!"

"Why did you hurt her?"

"You're a phony!"

All these little voices assailed me as I tried to revive the woman.

"Oh, no, she's fine. This is normal," I lied. The kids all crowded around me and their teacher who was lying unconscious on the floor.

"She's dead," one little voice cried.

"She's not dead," I insisted, perhaps a bit too loudly. "Look, she's moving. See? Dead people don't move."

"Wha . . . where . . . what happened?" Miss Spring stuttered.

"You had acupuncture," I reminded her. "You fainted."

"Oh. Ooooooh." Miss Spring looked around at all the alarmed faces staring at her. "Children, I'm fine. No need to worry."

"That's right," I joined in. "Sometimes, though not often, people faint. That's a normal response, but it is very rare. Miss Spring is a very unique person."

The kids looked at me with animosity in their eyes.

"Uh, any questions?" I asked.

Sophie, sometimes things just don't go the way we expect them to go. That's life. If we're lucky, they can at least make a good story.

IN THE MID-1980s, I got very depressed. Many of us get depressed at times, Sophie, and I think it is important to know this and accept it. Sometimes life just gets a person down. The older we get, and the more experience we have, the more we understand that this too shall pass. And it does, usually. But, when depression first hits us, it can seem so overwhelming that we can't see our way out of it. Believe me when I say that recovering from depression comes with experience and time. Be good to yourself and treat yourself with respect. You will find your way home again.

In the midst of this depression, I left my wonderful medical offices at Westbrook and Jann, the best medical partner with whom I could ever hope to work. After taking some time off, I went to a dilapidated clinic on the wrong side of the tracks where I worked with poverty stricken patients, many of whom had never had a doctor in their lives. When I look back now upon the whole situation, it seems absurd that I would want to leave my perfect office and partner.

I suppose I was burnt out. I was *the* doctor to the entire lesbian and gay community, always on-call to them even when I wasn't on-call. I felt I had to be medically perfect at all times because all the other doctors were looking at me through a magnifying glass, trying to discern ways to attack me. Once Jann came to the office, it was much better for me, but it was a bit too late for me to regain my early enthusiasm. Leaving the office was a way to get out from under all the pressure I was experiencing. So I thought. It was too bad, because in retrospect, I think I would have been much better off staying with Jann. But people who work as I do don't get away from the pressure. I still wanted to be perfect. I didn't want to give lesbians or lesbian doctors a bad name. I knew a lot of people relied on me and depended upon me. Although I loved that, I felt the pressure of it.

At this new clinic, I used to carry my stethoscope and other doctor "tools" in a brown paper bag and made daily house calls. Often, I had to climb up fire escapes, and enter apartments through a window. This was fun for maybe a week. But, these people needed my help, so I built up a big community clinic with services for them.

I MET DR. Katharina Dalton for the first time at a medical conference in the 1980s. She is the British doctor who coined the term PMS, PreMenstrual Syndrome. I was very interested in what she had to say and introduced myself to her. We got along well, and agreed to meet a few months hence at another conference in California. By then I had read a lot of what Dr. Dalton had written and, when we met again, I asked if I could come study with her in England for a short time because I wanted to set up a PMS Clinic in Calgary. At the time, PMS was quite controversial. In fact, most if not all of my colleagues thought I was crazy for wanting to get involved with PMS. I felt very confident that I was on the right track and that Dr. Dalton's theories were correct. I had a lot of patients whom I thought could be helped if diagnosed with PMS and given the correct treatment.

So, off I went to Harley Street in London, England where I spent several months with Dr. Dalton learning all about PMS. Those months were a wonderful time for me. During the days, I was at the Harley Street office and learned as much as I could. I stayed in a modest hotel nearby which wasn't fancy but it was comfortable enough. In the evenings, I went to the theatre or stayed in my room reading Agatha Christie books. I love learning, and Dr. Dalton was generous with her time, knowledge and information.

When I returned to Calgary I opened up Canada's first PMS Clinic. Almost immediately, we had more patients than I could handle and I had to start training others to help. And, also almost immediately, Jack, a fellow who had been in my residency years with me, wrote a letter to the College of Physicians and Surgeons and a letter to the editor of The Calgary Herald, the local newspaper, saying there was no such thing as PMS and Dr. Simkin was a charlatan and should immediately have her license revoked.

Once more, I had to defend myself to the College of Physicians and Surgeons of Alberta. I was glad of the lessons that Dr. Trueman had taught me about declaring myself and sticking up for what I believed. I was one of the few physicians in Canada at that time who believed that PMS was a real condition. The patients were another story. They came to see me with PMS symptoms that had plagued them for years. Using the knowledge I learned from Dr. Dalton in England, I was able to help them significantly. I think the doctors started to believe me after a few striking cases. For example, one young woman had been admitted to hospital every month for the last half a year. I was asked to see her and discovered that she was having severe PMS symptoms, which coincided with her hospital admissions. After I treated her, she was not admitted again.

Every department in the hospital has rounds, seminars where cases or different topics are presented and everyone can learn from them. And Grand Rounds takes place for everyone in the hospital and to present at Grand Rounds is a big thing. I was asked to give Grand Rounds on PMS and then I got more referrals and people started to believe me. After that I knew PMS had legitimate credibility.

Five years later, that very same Jack who demanded that my medical license be revoked and who was now a doctor in B.C., called me to ask if I would see a patient of his who was having a lot of trouble with PMS. He wasn't sure how to help her. Could I help her please? I wanted to ask him what he would have done had he been successful in having the College revoke my medical license. Who would have treated his patient then? But I didn't. I just took the information, saw the patient, fixed her up, and felt smug afterwards when I thought of him.

AS THE YEARS rolled by, I was definitely meeting some of my goals as a family physician. I remember the first time I delivered the baby of a woman whom I had delivered. The feeling I had then was overwhelming—positively overwhelming. It was wonderful.

After I had retired, I got an email from a young woman who wanted to have coffee with me. We met and it turned out I had delivered her. I remembered her mom well. She was now a medical resident and, from what I could tell, would make a wonderful doctor. I was so proud, although, truthfully, I had done nothing special. But that young woman made me feel so . . . fulfilled, maybe. Events like this come along during our lives, and we should relish and welcome them. These things are what it's all about. Well, what some of it is all about, at any rate.

1986
Twelve Years After Graduation

IN 1986, MY mother died. It was not unexpected. She had metastatic ovarian cancer following breast cancer, but her death was still very difficult for us all. In the months prior to her death, I would fly to Winnipeg for two extended week-ends every month and spend long hours on her bed talking with her. But, you know, Sophie, one never gets enough questions asked and experiences talked about when we are losing people we love. No matter how much we talk, there is always more to say and hear. I regretted not beginning years and years earlier, asking her so much more about her youth, her high school, her first job. So many things I want to know. Sophie, talk to your parents and grandparents. You may think you have all the time in the world to get answers to questions, but you never know what the future holds. Get as much information as possible. Keep doing it. Otherwise, you will wish you had. I regret not asking my grandmothers about their youth, about their experiences, their wisdom. I was young and thought I knew everything, or at least more than they did. I was so wrong. Please don't make the same mistake. Our foremothers have so much to teach us, we would be foolish not to learn from them, and all we have to do is listen.

When I returned to Calgary after the funeral, I was understandably very upset. As it turned out, there was a big rain storm my first night back after leaving my motherless family. I went outside and stood by my fence. The wind was howling, the rain pelting down as I clenched my hands on the top of the fence and screamed as loud as I possibly could. I screamed and screamed until I had screamed out some of the sorrow, at least for that moment. The wind was so loud, no one was able to hear me, even though I screamed until I was hoarse and could no longer talk. That night Mother Nature was my friend, helping me deal with my horrendous loss. The wind enveloped me and carried my agonized cry up into the heavens, looking for my mother's lost soul.

I have always had an affinity for wild nature, although admittedly, as I got older, my actions got progressively safer. I remember once being on a cruise with Maria. We were on a large ship, seven decks high. Off the coast of Mexico in the Bay of Tehuantepec, we ran into a gale. Passengers were advised to stay in our rooms, and the upper decks were closed. There were barf bags all over the stairwells, mostly unused. Maria was in bed, groaning as the boat lurched with the waves. She wasn't a great traveller under such circumstances. I, however, tracked down my new shipboard buddies (we'd already been on the ship several weeks) looking for an adventure. And an adventure we most definitely found.

First, we tied ropes very securely around our waists and each of us hitched up to two other partners, except for the first and last in line. Once we were all tightly tied one to another, we went up to the seventh deck and slowly pushed open the door. John, first in line, quickly lashed himself to the railing, and each of us, as we came outside, was immediately lashed securely to the railing. Once the five of us were all tightly attached, we leaned back and let it happen. And happen it did! Within seconds, we were drenched to the skin. The waves towered over us, rising up, crashing down upon us, over the top of our ship, seven stories high. It was terrifying and thrilling and totally mind blowing all at the same time.

"Yee-haw!" I yelled, in Calgary western fashion. We didn't stay out too long. It was very dangerous, and we would have been in a lot of trouble had we been discovered. But it was one of the most thrilling things I have ever done. Stupid, yes. But electrifying and exhilarating—absolutely!

Many years later, Maria and I did something that was also thrilling but much more appropriate to two older women. We rented a room at the Wickaninnish Inn in Tofino, on the west coast of Vancouver Island. It was March, storm season, and the hotel had rooms with windows from floor to ceiling, right over the ocean. We lay on the bed all day, watching the waves smash against the windows. It was magnificent, but did not make my heart beat quite as quickly as the experience on the ship.

The absolute power of Mother Nature is something very difficult to comprehend unless it is experienced. I hope, Sophie, that you never have to endure Mother Nature in one of her destructive modes. But she can be glorious to watch.

AROUND THIS TIME, I got interested in lasers and holograms. While at a medical conference in Eastern Canada, I had gone to a museum and seen a hologram exhibition. This interested me immensely. I found holograms just fascinating and shortly after I returned to Calgary, I found someone in California who could teach me how to make holograms. I went to a small town in northern California and learned about lasers and optic tables and holograms. And made my own holograms too.

When I came back to Calgary, I wanted to share my enthusiasm with everyone I knew. I thought holograms were just incredible and hoped others would too. In those days, I don't think I really knew how to do things in moderation; or at least, didn't want to. I rented a storefront in Mount Royal Village, a trendy area in Calgary, and opened Holomagic, Western Canada's first hologram gallery and store. I had art holograms—large wonderful pictures, and also sold what I used to call "holojunk": pins and belt buckles and necklaces and key chains and paperweights, things like that, all containing a hologram. The large holograms were amazing—one was a four foot square picture of jazz musician Dizzy Gillespie playing the trumpet. When one stood in the right place, the trumpet came out from the picture six feet. It was as though you could touch it, but it wasn't there.

The problem with these large holograms was that they all had to be lit exactly correctly with halogen lights at certain angles. Once everything was set up, they really were incredible, but it was not the kind of thing one could take home and easily replicate.

I sunk a lot of money into Holomagic and, for a short time, was very excited about it. But within the first year it became clear to me that I would much rather be practicing medicine and that, although I've always loved holograms, the world didn't necessarily share my enthusiasm. This was one of my projects that didn't do so well.

I had hired a business manager and within months, she told me she didn't want me in the gallery and shop during business hours. Her reason was that I gave away too many things and we weren't making enough money. Well, an art student would come in, admire something, and say, "Oh, I wish I could afford to buy that." And I would take it out of the display case and say, "Here, enjoy it." The smiles on their faces were worth the debits on the balance books to me. Not so to my business manager. I was banned. In my own gallery. I learned a lot about me, about money and business and, especially about other people.

But Sophie, I tried. I failed, but I did try, and that could be a good lesson. Don't be afraid to try things. Sometimes things will work, sometimes they won't. But even though Holomagic was not a roaring success, I still learned a lot about me, other people and the world. Never hold back from attempting something you like and want to do. We don't always succeed in life, but every experience has the potential to be a learning experience for us.

1989
Sixteen Years after Graduation

I WAS SITTING in my office when my phone buzzed.

"Teri is on the phone for you."

"Thanks. I'll take it now."

Teri was an old friend whom I had known since before I started medical school. She was very active with the pro-choice movement and active with CARAL, Canadian Abortion Rights Action League.

"Hi, Ruth. We have a big pro-choice rally in three weeks, to take place on the steps of the new City Hall. We're expecting a lot of people and wondered if you would do the main talk."

I sighed. More work for me. But good work for a good cause.

"Sure Teri, I'd be honoured. Thanks for asking."

After she gave me the details, I hung up and started thinking about what I might do for the rally.

The day arrived for the big pro-choice demonstration. There were many hundreds of people there, both pro-choice and pro-life. It was a cool day, a bit nippy, and the skies were clear blue with the odd white cloud. The new city hall of Calgary had wide steps leading up to the main doors. They had set the "stage" up on one of the stairs that was almost at the top. The podium was there with a microphone and, at the bottom of the stairs, people filled The Olympic Plaza. When it was my time to talk, I took hold of the microphone and stepped away from the dais.

"I, for one, am very grateful for the pro-choice movement, and for the hospitals where abortions are performed. As a doctor, I have seen far too many cases where abortions were not available to women. Do you know what women used to do, before we had the services we have now?"

I waited, and looked at the crowd. Then I pulled out a hanger from under my coat.

"This is what a woman had to do." I started straightening the hanger. I could hear mumbling and fidgeting in the audience. Once the hanger was fairly straight, I stood with my feet far apart and lowered the hanger.

"Can you imagine having to do this to yourself? Can you imagine it? This is what women had to do. They had to damage themselves with their unsterile hanger to get rid of an unwanted pregnancy." I had now brought the hanger down to my groin. There were murmurs in the audience. I carried on like that for quite some time. When I finished, by saying how much we should support our pro-choice movement, I lifted the straightened hanger high over my head and shouted, "This is not a surgical instrument!"

There was total silence. Just for a moment, but it seemed longer to me. Then the audience broke out into thunderous cheering and applause. I was pleased with the presentation.

I walked down the wide stairs to join my friends. Before I got to the last stair, I was surrounded by the pro-life people. They were furious at me, because I was known as a strong pro-choice advocate. They felt my presentation had been powerful and damaging to them, although I never mentioned them.

They started screaming at me, one woman in particular. It was Pat again, whom I knew as one of the leaders of the pro-life movement.

"You're going to hell! You are scum!"

Others joined in. "You're the worst kind of person to walk on this earth."

"'God will punish you."

"You go to hell!"

As they screamed at me, their rancour got louder and they got closer.

All of a sudden, my pro-choice buddies squeezed through them and formed a close circle around me. As the pro-life people still kept in their circle screaming at me, the pro-choice folks were quietly talking to me.

"Hang in there, Ruth."

"You're doing great, Ruth."

"It's just words."

So I was now in the centre of two circles, the pro-life people on the outside, shouting at me, while the pro-choice inside circle was talking quietly, reassuring me. I stood there, hands at my side, still holding my stretched-out hanger.

"Let them talk, they'll tire soon."

"Evil—you are so evil!"

"Devil! You are the devil incarnate!"

"Words, Ruth, it's just words. Ignore them."

I tried to stand there, calmly, shutting out the outer circle, and going inside myself. After about half an hour of this, people finally started to dissipate. I was so exhausted that I went home shortly after that.

Ending of 20th Century
beginning of 21st Century

IT SEEMED AS though I was as much involved in politics as in my medical practice, but they weren't necessarily separate. I started a yearly event, "From Woman to Woman: You and Your Health," where female doctors spoke about issues of interest to women in the community and answered questions at a full day seminar. It was highly successful, and as far as I know, is still going on many decades later.

Besides getting the Woman of the Year Award, I was also honoured with a Speak Sebastian award for lesbian and gay political activism. During my time in Calgary, I received many such accolades. I sat on numerous boards, took part on many panels, gave community lectures and still tried to maintain a full medical practice.

I remember the first time my father heard me speak publicly. I was giving a public lecture on some aspect of women's health and the place was packed. There were lots of questions, which I always encouraged. It was a very successful evening and, when it was over, my dad was just beaming.

"I didn't know you did that kind of thing," he gushed. "You were very good." That was an amazing thing for me, because my father didn't often give me compliments. He seemed puzzled that I could actually do this. "They all call you Doctor."

"Well, yeah, Dad, that's because I am one." I smiled back.

He was so blown away by the whole evening, but in a good way. I felt very proud that night.

But I was getting progressively tired and depressed, losing my balance in life. It was time for a change. At the time, Betty was in Vancouver studying advanced gynecological oncology and I decided to visit her. There was something about the coast that drew me. I loved living in Calgary, and loved the mountains but, after twenty-two years, my gut was telling me that perhaps the time had come to leave the mountains for the ocean. Maria and I had decided to end our relationship and there was nothing to keep me in Calgary. Although Betty would have been happy to share her apartment with me, I wanted to live with dogs and so got my own place in Vancouver. It felt right. Every day I would walk for hours with Wolfie, my wolf-cross dog, through the woods in the Endowment Lands near my home and, after a time, I felt my balance returning as I walked unencumbered in the world.

About this time, I found something that had been written by my friend, Neva, somewhere in my notes. I had realized, as I worked more and more in my medical office, how most women seemed to be subservient to medical doctors. This troubled me a lot and I worried about it at the time, wanting to be the kind of doctor patients enjoyed seeing and felt comfortable seeing. When I found what Neva had written, I was really delighted. It made me feel very good inside.

> I met Ruth when she was an intern. She was recommended by my friend Heather as "a great doctor." I had recently moved to Calgary and my last doctor was an aging "Rex Morgan," well meaning but condescending.
>
> Ruth was wearing a T-shirt (Mickey Mouse, I think), very thorough and efficient. I was so impressed and tongue-tied at the same time.
>
> She was giving me an internal examination and stopped and said, "Do you know what I am doing?" I said, "No," and she said, "Well, don't let people poke around with you if you don't know what they are doing." That was thirty years ago. I have never forgotten her words or their empowerment. She was doctor to me and my daughters until she stopped practicing in Calgary.

AFTER I HAD been in Vancouver for almost a year, Cory, my friend whom I had met twenty years earlier at Club Carousel in Calgary, came for a visit. She told me about a beautiful piece of land that was for sale on Salt Spring Island where she lived and offered to show me around.

I went, I saw, I bought. Ten and a half acres on the waterfront. I thought I would try farming for a while. I had always thought of farming as my second choice for an occupation.

I built a beautiful house on that property and built up a farm. I grew what I called yuppie vegetables: baby carrots, baby beets, fancy lettuces, many wonderful foods. I sold my produce to the local stores. My produce won ribbons several years in a row at the annual fall fair. I became a successful farmer. It was hard work and I liked it but, more and more, I missed medicine. No matter what I was doing, picking lettuce, weeding the artichokes, mounding the potatoes, I thought about my patients and my practice, with the odd thought going to the "fuckin' potatoes" of more than thirty years ago. No one on the island really even knew I was a doctor. I was just Ruth, the garlic farmer. But I wanted to be a doctor again.

I always had an interest in palliative care, except it wasn't called that when I worked in the hospital. Dying patients were almost always kept on medical wards and tended to be ignored there. But palliative care as a discipline was starting to become better known.

I knew the head of Family Medicine at the University of British Columbia and called her one day.

"I'm interested in palliative care, but I'm not sure what to do about it. Do you have any suggestions?"

"Oh, that's great, Ruth, because we were just thinking about starting a section of Palliative Care in our Family Medicine Department. You can be our first fellow."

And that is how I came to be the first person to do a Fellowship in Palliative Care at UBC. The Fellowship lasted two years and I worked in both Vancouver and Victoria. I loved it and felt so much better being back in medicine. I loved farming but, truthfully, I'm a much better doctor than I am a farmer. I loved my new field of Palliative Care. Hospices were now coming into existence in most cities. It wasn't really a new field, since of course people have been dying since the beginning of time. But, as a distinct and separate discipline, it was starting to come into its own.

After I finished my Fellowship at UBC, I went to the US to write my specialty exams. Canada included Palliative Care with Family Medicine but, in the US, one could become a licensed specialist in the field. That is what

I did. I passed my specialty certification exams and returned to Salt Spring Island with a lot more initials after my name.

Since Victoria was a thirty-five minute ferry ride away from Salt Spring Island, I rented a room in a small house near the hospital in Victoria. I started working at the Hospice in Victoria as a staff physician and felt as though I had come home. It was one of the best jobs I ever had. First of all, I was accepted as a doctor. At the Hospice, everyone practiced just the way the Calgary School of Medicine indicated they wanted medicine to be: respectful, caring, loving. I adored my job and my colleagues were wonderful to work with. Other than being on call, I was done after my shift. I was not overly active in the community, at least not yet. I felt as though I was in paradise.

I had two wonderful animals, Wolfie and Lupie. They were sisters but Wolfie was from a litter born a year earlier than Lupie. Their mom was a gorgeous white, Arctic wolf and their dad, a black Belgian Shepherd. They were beautiful creatures, both over one hundred pounds, and as gentle as could be.

I trained them well and they used to come to work with me. The Hospice patients loved them and, if they weren't with me, asked for them. They would lie under the desk in my office and, when I made rounds, they would often accompany me. They were able to jump up on a bed and have the patient cuddle or pet them without hurting the patient at all. They were so gentle. They instinctively knew what to do.

One day, I was sitting down by the elevator after a long day. I was tired. A young woman left one of the rooms down the hall, slammed the door, and ran to the bank of chairs where I was sitting. She had both her hands over her face and was crying hysterically. I usually knew everyone who came to the ward but I didn't know her, so I just sat quietly. But Wolfie knew better. She very slowly walked up to the woman and just stood in front of her. The woman took her hands off her face. Wolfie started to lick the tears rolling down her cheeks. The woman put her arms around Woflie's neck and cried, "Oh, you wonderful dog, you." And she sobbed into her neck. Wolfie stood still.

Eventually the elevator came. Lupie and I got up and walked into the elevator. Wolfie gave the woman one last lick and followed. That woman smiled at Wolfie, no doubt comforted by that little interlude.

There were many such episodes. I have had dog companions now for more than fifty-five years, always training them well. They usually came with me to work if possible. My current companion, Kelly, is a Golden Doodle whom I have trained to be a service dog. Kelly helps me with many things around the house, but mostly she makes me laugh every day. Every one of my animal companions has been special, starting way back with Peppy the Poodle and Jennifer the Saint Bernard. I can't imagine living without a dog. A person, yes, I can imagine living without a person. And I do. But a dog—never. My animal companions have always played a very important role in my life.

As time went on, I found it progressively difficult commuting between my home on Salt Spring Island and my work in Victoria. I didn't have much of a life either on the island or in the city, as it seemed I was always going or coming. It was time for another big decision.

On Salt Spring, I had built my dream home. My property there was truly exceptional and I designed and built a house that would be perfect for me even as I got older and my body became more frail. I agonized over the big decision: should I stay in my beautiful home on Salt Spring or move to Victoria and completely commit to my work at the Hospice working in Palliative Care? Ultimately medicine won. No more commuting. No more managing a farm where I didn't even work anymore. The thought of getting up in the morning every day and going to work at the Hospice was just too tempting. I did what I wanted to do.

I bought a house in Victoria, not quite like my Salt Spring dream house, but wonderful just the same. For five years I worked there, loving every second of it. Sophie, you would be surprised at how much one could learn about living from spending time with the dying. It was such a privilege to be able to do that work. I loved everything about it.

When I first came to Victoria, I didn't know anyone here other than the people at work. There is a synagogue in Victoria, Congregation Emanu-el. I found out it was the oldest functioning synagogue in all of Canada. I thought to myself: what if I should suddenly die? No one even knows me; I have no community. I need to do something about that. So, one day I went to the synagogue. The people there were so friendly and welcoming, and in no time, I was involved with projects there, including sitting on the board of directors for several years. I took over publishing the Victoria Jewish Community Directory. And, I had a community. Things were good again.

This time I didn't get quite so frustrated or burnt out combining medical work, politics, and community service. I'm sure a big reason for that was maturity and a different perception of my place in the world.

You know, Sophie, we do what we can. Sometimes we feel we have to fix things absolutely, but that may simply not be possible. I often remind myself of one of my favourite stories and I hope you carry it with you throughout your life. It goes like this:

Not long ago, there was a huge storm on the west coast. It was Mother Nature at her wildest, and trees were pulled out of the ground, water splashed everywhere, including places it shouldn't be.

The day after the storm was a beautiful day, a calmness in the air, sun shining, almost as though nothing had happened the day before. Except the beach was just a wreck. There were starfish everywhere on the sand where they had been tossed by the waves. They needed to be in the water to survive. An elderly woman was slowly making her way down the beach, picking up starfish and throwing them back into the water.

A young man walked onto the beach and sat on a log. He watched the old woman laboriously throw the starfish back into the water. He looked up and down the beach at the absolute havoc that the storm had wreaked. He shook his head at the devastation of the beach but, even more, at the old woman. When he could no longer stand it, he ran up to her and put his hand out, as if to stop her.

"What are you doing, you crazy lady! There are thousands and thousands of starfish on the beach. You will never save them all. Can't you see that what you are doing is making no difference?"

The woman stopped her work and smiled at the young man.

"Nonsense," she said as she picked up another starfish. As she threw it into the ocean, she looked again at the young man. "It made a difference to that one," and she bent over and picked up another one and threw it into the water, "and it makes a difference to this one," and she picked up another to throw in the water, "and this one, and this one . . ." And she continued her way down the beach, saving what she could.

I realized I couldn't do it all. I never could when I was younger, but at least now I realized how ludicrous it was to even try. By the time I was working in Victoria, I was doing what I could. Hopefully it made a difference for that one, and another one. I couldn't save or help everyone. That's not even the point. I think the point is to do the best we can with our lives. If we help living beings as we walk through life, so much the better. But we can only do what we can do. No more than that. I hope you realize that at a much younger age than I when I first understood. The starfish lady is never far from my thoughts. I try to use her as a good example of doing what we can.

At about this time, for several months I flew to Calgary on week-ends. In one of life's more ironic moments, Betty, that brilliant gynecological oncologist, was now back in Calgary dying of gynecological cancer. She was a very close friend and I wanted to be with her as much as I could. Also, she wasn't eating much those days but she loved the French toast I used to make for her. So I would fly into Calgary, drive off to a special bakery for particularly good bread, and go to her house which she now rarely left and I would make her French toast. And we would eat our meal and talk. Sometimes we would just sit together in silence. Most times I would think about how life just is not fair. Of all people, why Betty? She was an expert in her field and one of the kindest, smartest, gentlest people I knew. I still miss her very much. One of the most significant prices we pay for getting older, for living longer, is having to say goodbye to people we love.

"I thought spines were supposed to be straight."
My sister tipped her head to the side as she studied the x-ray.
"Correct. Most spines are straight." The doctor raised his eyebrows at her.
"But this spine is like a question mark. It's anything but straight!"
"That's right. And that is why we are telling you that your sister has very serious spinal disease. This is one of the worst curvatures I have seen."
"Well, what will happen?"
"Hey, you two, I am here, you know," I interrupted, feeling that this conversation about my body was taking place without any input from me except for my ridiculously sinuous spine up there on the lit x-ray box.
"Sorry," they both said at once.
The doctor sat on a table, one knee up, his arm leaning across it. He turned to my sister. "Ruth and I have discussed this; because of this spinal disease, she will lose inches in height . . ."

"I've already lost close to five inches," I interrupted.

"That's because the disease has caused the spaces between the vertebrae to disappear. This also means that the nerves will be compressed, and she might notice numbness and tingling or loss of sensation in hands, or legs. She will also start to have more pain with this."

"I already have all that."

Judi just shook her head.

As we were leaving the doctors' office after a long consultation, she turned to me. "I had no idea. No idea at all. It's pretty bad, isn't it?"

"Well, yeah, I guess, but you know, it's certainly better than the alternative." She shot me a questioning look.

"I'd rather be here with a bad spine, and some numbness in my hands and feet and a bit of pain, than not be here at all. So I'll take it. The alternative is being dead, and I don't want to be dead. At least not for a long time."

"You really have had a tough time—first you had all those stomach surgeries, and then all that stuff with your pituitary gland not working, and now this. And really, it's not *just* a little bit of pain or a little numbness, is it? Aren't you angry?"

"No, not really. Like I said, it's better than the alternative. Would I rather be pain free and have a normal spine? Sure. But I don't, so why worry about it? It is what it is."

And that, Sophie, has always been my attitude towards my body and my health. I have had far more illnesses than most. It's sort of ironic since I have spent a good part of my life eradicating illness in others. I wish I could do the same for me, but that does not seem possible. So rather than dwell on all the things that happen to me, I choose to ignore them as much as I safely can and live my life the best I am able, given my limitations. I hope you never become ill, or develop a chronic disease, but if you do, integrate it into your life the best way you know how, treat yourself well, don't dwell on it, and live to the best of your abilities. Too many people spend their hours worrying about what was or what is, and talk about being ill *ad nauseum* to the exclusion of anything else. They have given up on their lives. Don't ever do that. It's not necessary. Accept what your life brings you and remember, you are still here, still living, and that's a real gift. We can be dead for all of eternity, so we might as well enjoy the little bit of time we do get. If it comes with diseases, so be it. It still comes.

It is interesting to me how one thing morphs into another. We have to be open to change. I used to be a gourmand omnivore; now I am a happy vegan. I just could not use animals any longer for my own benefits and especially to their detriment. It's always a surprise what life has in store for us and we should be open to it all. And learn from our experiences.

When I first became a feminist over fifty years ago, one of the first things of which I was aware was the language—the language I had been using my whole life was disrespectful to women or left women out of the language all together. Today I am very aware of language and when I hear "he" when the author really means "he and she" or even just "she," my blood still boils. Of course, the language, as sexist as it was and unfortunately still is, is only a very small part of society's ignoring one half of the population. The fact that women are still not equal in so many ways—equal pay for equal work, for example, these are the important things. Feminism is really true equality between women and men; nothing more, and nothing less.

There are many people who scoff at the word "feminism." But consider this—when I was in my first year of medical school, I, and any other woman, could not get a credit card in our own name. Until 1974, a husband's signature was needed for women to have credit cards. At that time, I met women who were teachers who lost their jobs because they and their husbands wanted to start a family and they became pregnant—a no-no for working teachers until 1978. I could go on and on with examples like this to show why feminism was, and still is, such an important part of all our lives.

One day I was getting ready to go to work at the Hospice and did not feel so well. I called in and told the receptionist I would be back in a day or two. Two days later I called again to say I would be back to work the following week. The week stretched into a month, then months, and I did not go back to work. Ever again. My body had finally succumbed to the illnesses I had been trying unsuccessfully to deal with. I retired from the Hospice, unwillingly, but knowing it was necessary because of my health problems.

After I left the Hospice, I went into a depression again. I missed working there so much. I had always wanted to write so, together with another newly retired Hospice doctor and four women who were complete strangers, we formed a writing group. I wrote a book about my experiences in the mental hospital, published in 2010, *The Jagged Years of Ruthie J.* It got very good reviews across the country. I discovered that I loved writing and subsequently have had several more books published.

The lesson I learned here, Sophie, and one which I hope you will keep in mind, is that there is always something possible for one to do. For me at this point in my life, it is writing. For you, it may be something else. And these somethings change throughout our lives. Before writing, I was a Palliative Care specialist. I loved that. And now, I'm a writer. I love that. And if or when I can no longer write, I will find something else to love. We can't always do what we want to do, but there is no reason we can't do something we love to do. Even if it is just being kind to other people.

These days I rarely go to the synagogue or anywhere else for that matter. I no longer work as a physician. My body does not work as well as I would like it to. I am wheelchair-bound now and doing almost anything is very labour intensive. I can't drive, can't walk, can't do many of the things I loved to do. One of the biggest things I miss is walking with my dog. When I lived with Reenie, the wolf/husky cross I had before Kelly, we walked in the woods for hours every day. That was such a special time for me.

One day I got terribly lost in the woods. I had fallen, my knee was bleeding and I was generally feeling sorry for myself. I had no idea where I was or how to get home. I sat down on a rock. As I wiped the blood off my knee and the tears off my cheeks, I looked at Reenie and whimpered, "Take me home please, Reenie, I'm so lost. I don't know where we are. Please get me home." She licked my face, turned around, and started walking. I followed. Within twenty minutes, we were walking through our front door.

Now I go out with Kelly but I am in my wheelchair or scooter. Modern times are so different. My watch has a GPS. There are so many electronics that help us out. However, I really have to say that, as helpful as they are, I kinda liked the old ways better. Take, for example, travelling. When I travelled in the 60s, 70s, and 80s, there were no cell phones or email. I would call home from China once a month, and write letters by hand. If I had a problem I had to solve it on my own. These days, it is almost as though people aren't even away. They are in constant touch, complete with videos, with everyone they know. There is less sense of adventure now. I hope, Sophie, you are able to experience some of that sense of adventure, safely, of course, but on your own, without everyone overwhelming you with their opinions. You can indeed exist in the world without the help of electronics, using your own brain and common sense.

The lesson here is to always trust yourself. Get as much information as you can from other people, but do what feels right for you. If something feels wrong, or out of place, examine it very carefully. There will always be down times. There always are, irrevocably, in everyone's life. But even in the midst of a down time, your essence is still there somewhere. Possibly depression or inertia is covering it up, but it is there. Find it. Trust your native goodness. Whoever you are—be *that* person. You can make lots of changes throughout life but be true to whomever you are at any one time. Believe yourself. Believe *in* yourself.

I've always loved sharing stories, both hearing them from others and telling them myself. Stories transform us, they empower us. Sophie, I hope my sharing stories with you will help you to live a fulfilled, happy life. I certainly have had a full life. Just the other day I got an email from Rob, the very same Rob I met in 1969 at Club Carousel and who has been my friend throughout all these years. He was reminiscing a bit and this is part of what he wrote:

> We still talk of all the wonderful times and experiences that only you brought to our lives . . . you showed us white water rafting, hot air ballooning, helicopters over Manhattan, horse back riding, 50s parties, nude croquet, wonderful meals and parties, stories from China . . . you taught us all to laugh, you gave us love, you shared all of your wonderful animals. You shared the maze in your yard. I watched you play burro polo in Mexico, we wore pink wigs to the Acropolis in Greece . . . I can go on forever.

So you see, Sophie, there are still many more stories I could tell you, but perhaps you've heard enough. I'm an old woman now and I have enjoyed a very full life. But this is not so much about the life I have had, Sophie, but rather about the life you are about to have. I so hope you allow yourself to be a whole person, honest with yourself and others. I hope perhaps some of what I've told you here will remain with you and you will think about other women in society and help to better our position as I have done. My wish for you is that you grow up to be a strong, forceful woman, who is also gentle and kind and understanding. Learn as much as you can about anything you can. Knowledge is always helpful. You can never learn too much. But remember, Sophie, true wisdom does not come only from book learning. Gather all the wisdom and knowledge you can. Just keep it all inside you; everything will become apparent when it needs to. I know I will be very proud of you, Sophie. I encourage you to be your beautiful self, no matter what that takes. In the long run, it will be worth it.

You and the women of your generation are the reason that I and the women of my generation worked so hard. And I sincerely hope that you and your cohorts do the same for the next generations.

And above all Sophie, have fun, laugh, enjoy life. Look for the wonder and the beauty that is around you. Embrace life fully. Keep my stories with you.

With love, Auntie Ruth

Ruth Simkin's published books include *What Makes You Happy*, a book of short stories, T*he Jagged Years of Ruthie J*, a memoir which met with critical acclaim, *Like an Orange on a Seder Plate, a Feminist Haggadah*, and *The Y Syndrome*. She has written countless medical papers and contributed to textbooks, as well as doing many mixed media presentations. She has published many non-medical articles and booklets on a variety of topics.

She currently lives with her Golden Doodle, Kelly, and when she is not writing, is contentedly reflecting on the ocean, the flora and the wildlife around her home.